UNPACKING FAKE NEWS

UNPACKING FAKE NEWS

An Educator's Guide to Navigating the Media with Students

EDITED BY
Wayne Journell

Foreword by Rebecca Klein
Afterword by Jeremy Stoddard

TEACHERS COLLEGE PRESS
TEACHERS COLLEGE | COLUMBIA UNIVERSITY
NEW YORK AND LONDON

Published by Teachers College Press, 1234 Amsterdam Avenue, New York, NY 10027

Front cover photo by MirageC / Getty Images.

Library of Congress Cataloging-in-Publication Data is available at loc.gov

ISBN 978-0-8077-6114-4 (paper)
ISBN 978-0-8077-6115-1 (hardcover)
ISBN 978-0-8077-7758-9 (ebook)

Printed on acid-free paper
Manufactured in the United States of America

26 25 24 23 22 21 20 19 8 7 6 5 4 3 2 1

Contents

Foreword

When Donald Trump first began tweeting the term *fake news* in December 2016, during that hazy time when he had not yet taken office but the country felt on the verge of a seismic shift, I thought it was only a matter of months before the term would reach its colloquial expiration date. I imagined it becoming a puzzling relic that would mark one of the strangest points in American history. I did not suspect that it would become a term which, 2 years later, is still carrying weight and used as a defense by the powerful and desperate alike.

Like the man who popularized it, the term has had staying power. It is a term that, for a reporter like myself, can be akin to the sound of nails on a chalkboard. Sometimes I am personally called "fake news" in the form of an email from a critical reader. Other times my articles are called "fake news" in the form of a tweet from an impolite, unidentifiable user. The reader might think the reported news is legitimately made up or feel that it simply reflects a worldview with which they disagree. The hurler of this invective is usually older and often appears to be someone who has long been out of school.

It may be too late for the readers who call me "fake news" to consume the news with a more discerning eye—or for the news media to gain back their trust. (Indeed, there are certainly many reasons to distrust the media right now, and there are many times the media gets it wrong.) But that does not mean there is no hope for the future.

While, sadly, only about 44% of teenagers say they feel confident in their ability to distinguish between real news and patently made-up "fake news" (Common Sense Media, 2017), the techniques outlined in this book give me hope that educators will be able to beat back the epidemic of news illiteracy that infects so much of this country. In order for us to do better, we not only need a profession composed of good journalists, but we also need a society of informed consumers that will hold journalists to account in thoughtful ways and fairly hold our feet to the fire. I imagine a future where readers are not only more informed, but also one where future journalists know how to avoid some of the pitfalls of the past.

Inside this book you will find a thorough explanation of what "fake news" is, how it became such a phenomenon, and why we are so susceptible to believing it. You will find descriptions of simple lessons practiced by experts that can help make students more critical news consumers. You will hear from a variety of perspectives, some of which are sadly still too often overlooked in mainstream narratives. You may even learn that you have not been reading news with the most judicious eye.

Indeed, there are already so many reasons to be excited about how kids of today will improve the world they are inheriting. If we have learned anything from recent events, like the aftermath of the tragic school shooting in Parkland, Florida, it is that today's teens already know how to use social media to spread information for good. They have shown that they can be startlingly powerful when they are armed with facts and filled with passion. Having grown up on the Internet, getting news from Tumblr posts and Reddit threads, they are used to navigating digital challenges that may seem foreign to older adults.

It would be nice to live in a world where "fake news" was not a problem and those in power did not try to discredit any reporting that might reflect an unflattering truth. But that is not our reality. The chapters in this book are instructional in describing what the current problems are, where they came from, and where we can go from here.

Our democracy could depend on it.

—Rebecca Klein

REFERENCE

Common Sense Media. (2017, March 8). New report: Kids value the news media but feel misrepresented, neglected by coverage. Retrieved from www.commonsensemedia.org/about-us/news/press-releases/new-report-kids-value-the-news-media-but-feel-misrepresented-neglected

Preface

I did not plan to publish this book. I had just published three books in the span of 2 years, and honestly, I was tired. Yet, like many people across the United States, the result of the 2016 presidential election took me by surprise and shook me to my core. As an adult, I have come to realize that many people do not share my views of the world and that part of living in a democracy is learning to accept election results that do not go my way. However, at no point in my life had I ever witnessed an election that made me concerned about the civic well-being of our nation.

As a civic education scholar, I felt I had to do *something* about the civic illiteracy that led to the election of someone like Donald Trump, but I did not know what. In all honesty, I remained shell shocked for quite a while after the election. However, little by little, I started seeing exceptional articles being published—many of which were authored by the scholars in this book—that were confronting the problem of "fake news" head on. Yet they were being published in disparate venues—a social studies journal here, a generalist journal there, the occasional book chapter. Therefore, I decided that my contribution to this effort would be to collect all of this great work in one place.

The contributors to this volume, many of whom I am proud to call colleagues, are the stars of this show. They are doing amazing, important work, and I am beyond grateful that they agreed to take part in this endeavor. I am also indebted to Brian Ellerbeck at Teachers College Press for seeing the potential in this work, particularly as it landed on his desk in an unconventional manner! In all our interactions, I have found Brian responsive, straightforward, and affable, and he has made this experience with Teachers College Press an extremely positive one. The rest of the Teachers College Press team has also been wonderful to work with, especially Lori Tate and Nancy Power who were so attentive in the production and marketing of the book. I would also like to thank Rebecca Klein of *HuffPost* for agreeing to write the foreword and providing a journalistic context to the educational approaches contained in this book.

From a personal standpoint, this book would not have come together without the support I receive from my family and my colleagues at the University of North Carolina at Greensboro. Specifically, I would like to thank my wife, Kitrina, for always allowing me to vent about politics at home and my parents, Allen and Brenda, for their constant encouragement. Finally, as with all my professional endeavors, I dedicate this book to my daughter, Hadleigh, who will be entering kindergarten by the time it is published. Like most parents, I worry about the world in which she will grow up, but this book is evidence that there will always be hard-working professionals dedicated to making our schools and society a little better than they were before, and as a parent, I am comforted by that fact.

Introduction

Fake News and the Imperative of Civic Education

Wayne Journell

In 2017 the lexicographers at Collins Dictionary, a publication of the distinguished HarperCollins publishing house, named "fake news" as its word of the year. Although determining words of the year is fairly subjective, research has shown that these words often reflect the cultural zeitgeist of a specific time in history (Heafner, Triplett, Handler, & Massey, 2018). "Fake news" is no exception.

Beginning with his victory in the 2016 Republican presidential primary and then throughout the subsequent general election campaign, Donald Trump used the term *fake news* to dismiss negative stories written about him by the "mainstream" media. The tactic worked; multiple surveys taken in the wake of the 2016 election and the first year of Trump's presidency have shown that Republicans—particularly those who identify as Trump supporters—distrust the mainstream media and do not support its role as a government watchdog (e.g., Barthell & Mitchell, 2017; The Economist, 2017; Guess, Nyhan, & Reifler, 2017; Swift, 2016).

Many mainstream media outlets have responded by asserting their legitimacy and making a case for their role in a healthy democracy. *The Washington Post*, for example, adopted the slogan "democracy dies in darkness," early in 2017 (Concha, 2017b), and *The New York Times* followed suit with their own proclamation that "the truth is more important than ever" (Concha, 2017a). Many Internet-based news outlets, such as HuffPost, have also recently taken steps to bolster their journalistic reputations and minimize unvetted stories due to the prevalence of actual fake news online (Lima, 2018).

Trump has continued his defamation of the media throughout the start of his presidency. From December 2016, one month after winning the election, to the start of the following December, Trump tweeted about fake news over 150 times (Coll, 2017), and he continues to use the term on a regular basis to admonish news organizations with whom he disagrees, even when confronted with verifiable facts. From a political standpoint, the purpose behind Trump's branding of mainstream media as fake news "has been to relentlessly turn questions of fact into questions of motive" (Friedman, 2017, para. 7).

An illustrative example can be found during Trump's diplomatic trip to Great Britain in 2018. While in Britain, he gave an interview to the British newspaper *The Sun,* in which he criticized British Prime Minister Theresa May, specifically her handling of the Brexit issue (Dunn, 2018). The following day, at a press conference with May, Trump accused *The Sun* of publishing a biased account that did not present accurate comments from the interview. Trump stated that the article was fake news, that he "did not criticize the prime minister," and that he would release an audio recording of the interview to show that *The Sun* was taking his words out of context (Blake, 2018, para. 2). *The Sun*, however, then released their own audio of the interview which clearly showed Trump criticizing May for her handling of Brexit. Yet neither Trump nor The White House issued any retraction of Trump's claim that *The Sun* interview was fake news (Blake, 2018; Croucher, 2018).

By regularly blurring the line between fact and opinion, Trump has given license for people to dismiss information that contradicts their preexisting worldviews while simultaneously accepting verifiable untruths because they reinforce a broader ideology and/or sense of purpose. Moreover, this admonishment of the mainstream media has occurred alongside the rise of hyper-partisan media outlets, increasing political polarization, and a greater ability than ever before for people to self-select the media they consume. This combination has the potential for grave civic consequences, both in the United States and, increasingly, throughout the world (Friedman, 2017).

It is worth noting that Americans' distrust of media and their willingness to ignore facts in pursuit of their ideological convictions were occurring well before Trump entered the political arena (e.g., Arceneaux, Johnson, & Murphy, 2012; Gunther, 1992; Hochschild & Einstein, 2015; Lee, 2005). Moreover, Trump is far from the only contemporary politician to fabricate stories, and his supporters are not the only ones to dismiss facts in pursuit of ideological certainty. For example, in a 2012 interview President Obama attributed the controversial "Fast and Furious" program, which allowed for the selling of guns to members of drug cartels in Mexico, to his predecessor, George W. Bush. That statement was later determined to be false (Drobnic Holan & Sherman, 2012). More recently, liberals who were upset at the Trump administration's policy of separating families attempting to enter the United States illegally took to social media to voice their displeasure, often posting pictures of children locked in cages. Yet many of these images were of children who had been separated from their families during the Obama administration (Borchers, 2018).

It is evident, however, that Trump has turned the notion of fake news—both as a method of pushing an ideology and as a strategy for dismissing inconvenient truths—into a political weapon. Trump and his supporters' brazen disregard for facts, coupled with a social media landscape that allows for the repetition of untruths within self-selected echo chambers, suggests that American society may have begun a descent from which it will be impossible to recover.

For those who are not yet ready to write off American democracy as we know it, education may be the key to halting its decline. Although media literacy has been taught in K–12 schools for decades, the premise that factual information could be considered illegitimate simply because it contradicts one's worldview presents new challenges for educators. The remainder of this introduction will elaborate on how we are defining fake news in this book before ending with a brief description of how the subsequent chapters both help explain the civic consequences of fake news and offer suggestions for addressing it in K–12 classrooms.

DEFINING FAKE NEWS[1]

At the heart of the democratic process is the belief that the polity will establish a system of governance that is fair to all members of society. Of course, fairness is subjective, and it is incumbent upon the collective members of the polity to determine what is fair through an open deliberative process that allows for a range of rational viewpoints (Gutmann & Thompson, 2004; Habermas, 1962/1989). Moreover, for a democratic society to protect the rights of all citizens, it is essential that people move beyond simply advocating for policies that protect their own self interests. Rather, a healthy democracy is one that adopts policies based on reason, evidence, and the strongest arguments (Habermas, 1981/1984; Rawls, 1993).

Thus, it is widely acknowledged among democratic theorists that without an informed citizenry, democracy cannot flourish (e.g., Delli Carpini & Keeter, 1996; Dewey, 1916; Mill, 1859/1975). Perhaps even more disastrous for democracy is a citizenry informed with erroneous information that cannot discern truth from fiction or fact from opinion. Misinformation masquerading as fact affects the very foundations of our democratic process.

From a civic standpoint, then, one of the major ramifications of Trump's appropriation of the term *fake news* is that it has drawn attention from actual fake news—information that is verifiably false. Moreover, Trump's success in getting people to automatically assume that news that contradicts their ideological beliefs is fake has made actual fake news more believable and thus more prevalent and effective. When individuals lose the willingness or ability to vet their political information, democracy is at risk.

The Russian attempt to influence the 2016 election is an illustrative example of the inherent dangers of actual fake news. According to U.S. intelligence agencies, the Russian government sought to swing the election in favor of Trump, in part through a calculated dissemination of fraudulent information on social media (The Washington Post, 2017). Although the extent to which the Russian-sponsored propaganda influenced the outcome of the election is unclear, Russian operatives posted approximately 80,000 pieces of propaganda on Facebook alone that were then shared by social media users, ultimately reaching approximately 126 million people (Isaac & Wakabayashi, 2017; Shapiro, 2017).

For the purposes of this book, then, it is important to clearly delineate between Trump's version of fake news and the actual fake news that presents a threat to democracy. For Trump and his supporters, accusations of fake news are usually about *bias* and not fact, whereas in this book we are focusing on actual fake news—factually inaccurate information being presented as fact.

Bias

Bias in news reporting is not new; in fact, in the early part of the 19th century, U.S. newspapers were expected to present partisan viewpoints (Schudson, 1978). Identifying and understanding bias is an essential component of both political and media literacy. Yet bias does not necessarily equate to fraudulent information; rather, it is about how factual information is interpreted and presented. A liberal news outlet and a conservative news outlet can take drastically different positions on a given issue, but both could be factually accurate.

Consider, for example, the various analyses around the Tax Cuts and Jobs Act of 2017 passed by Republican majorities in Congress and signed into law by President Trump. Liberal-leaning publications, such as *The New York Times* and *The Washington Post,* offered analyses suggesting that the law would primarily benefit corporations and the top one percent of earners (Cohen, 2017; Fischer-Baum, Soffen, & Long, 2018), whereas conservative-leaning publications, such as *The Wall Street Journal* and *The Washington Times*, argued that the law would lead to economic growth for all Americans, particularly the middle class (Kudlow, 2017; Moore, 2017).

Despite the different conclusions that were drawn, all of these mainstream media outlets were operating with the same basic facts (i.e., scoring by the Congressional Budget Office). Although Trump and his surrogates called the liberal analyses of the tax plan fake news (e.g., Giaritelli, 2017; Gingrich, 2017), such accusations would not meet the definition of fake news we are using in this book. Different interpretations of factual content are not harmful for democracy; on the contrary, a healthy democracy relies on the deliberation of competing rational viewpoints on open controversial issues (Hess & McAvoy, 2015).

It is important, however, to have *all* of the facts. Mainstream news outlets, particularly cable news and other television-based news outlets, have contributed to the rise of fake news by emphasizing certain stories over others and watering down complex issues into sound bites. News networks have become corporate entities, and news directors realize that the most effective way to increase viewership (and thus profits) is to consistently present clear partisan narratives. It is common knowledge in the United States, for example, that Fox News caters to conservative viewers and MSNBC pushes a liberal perspective. As a result, many liberals will automatically discredit a story on Fox News, as conservatives will for an MSNBC story, without even reading/viewing it, even though both outlets generally report factually accurate stories.

While prominent media outlets like Fox News and MSNBC have well-known ideological leanings, other forms of news bias are not as transparent. Take, for example, Sinclair Media Group, which is the owner of the largest number of television stations in the United States. The corporation has a far-right agenda, but instead of advocating for that agenda in overt ways like one might see on Fox News, Sinclair uses local television news programs to subtly push its agenda on unsuspecting viewers. Sinclair forces all of its television stations to run the same news stories, often requiring anchors to read off a script, ensuring that viewers across the country will receive the same news in the same way (Graves, 2017).

A final way that mainstream news outlets have helped set the stage for the rise of actual fake news is through their practice of reducing complex information into simplistic terms that likely support the political narrative to which they prescribe. While it is the responsibility of news networks to make information accessible to consumers, too often these efforts result in sound bites that lack a critical understanding of the entire issue at hand. These stories are factual and may even be backed by research or other forms of data, but they commit the sin of omission, leading consumers to form opinions based on incomplete information. Assuming the simplistic narrative fits within their worldview, consumers are likely to accept it without attempting to inquire into the complexities of the issue.

Actual Fake News

While bias in news reporting is problematic, particularly as Americans increasingly retreat into self-selected ideological echo chambers, it is when one's viewpoints are shaped by incorrect facts that democracy is truly threatened. Following the 2016 presidential election, several graphs and other types of visuals were widely circulated on social media in an attempt to educate people about the differences between legitimate, fraudulent, and biased news outlets (for examples of these visuals, see Journell, 2018; North Idaho College, 2018). Given that many of these visuals were not created by political scientists or experts in journalism or communication, none of them should be considered definitive assessments of the quality or ideological stances of news outlets. However, these visuals are illustrative in that there is considerable overlap among them, despite the ideological differences of their authors.

Regardless of the ideological convictions of the authors, all of the visuals describe traditional, mainstream news outlets such as *The New York Times, The Wall Street Journal,* and *Politico* (i.e., outlets that Trump regularly refers to as "fake news") as publications in which readers can access factual news reporting and high-quality analysis. The authors' ideological differences only become apparent when they place news outlets along a liberal/conservative spectrum. Some of the liberal authors, for example, describe outlets like CBS News, NBC News, and National Public Radio as "neutral" outlets, whereas conservative authors tend to describe them as having a liberal slant.

For the purposes of this book, we are more concerned with outlets that are perceived to peddle fraudulent information. Consider, for example, InfoWars, which is identified as a poor-quality news source on all of the visuals that circulated on social media following the 2016 presidential election. InfoWars is primarily a medium for the conspiracy theories of its founder, Alex Jones, a conservative radio host. Here are just a few of the theories that have been championed by Jones and InfoWars in the past (Hanna, 2017; Madsen, 2016; Quigley, 2017):

> The 9/11 attacks on the World Trade Center and Pentagon, the 2012 Sandy Hook Elementary School shooting, and the 1995 Oklahoma City bombing were orchestrated by the U.S. government.
>
> Former President Barack Obama is the "global head" of Al-Qaeda.
>
> The U.S. government is using juice boxes and city-controlled water supplies to turn people gay.
>
> Former Supreme Court Justice Antonin Scalia was murdered.

While it would be easy to dismiss such baseless accusations as fodder from a crazy person, doing so would ignore the over two million people who tune into his weekly radio show and the countless others who visit InfoWars.com or watch his videos that circulate on social media (Southern Poverty Law Center, 2018). Trump has also given InfoWars legitimacy; as a candidate for president, he appeared on Jones's radio show, praising the host's "amazing" reputation (Bradner, 2015, para. 2), and retweeted a post from a top InfoWars editor (Savransky, 2016). While in office, he allegedly has contacted Jones for advice (Rutenberg, 2017).

From a pedagogical standpoint, it would be tempting to just tell students that InfoWars is actual fake news and that they should get their information from mainstream media outlets. Such an approach, however, is too simplistic. Creating a dichotomous "good" versus "bad" distinction does not allow for the possibility that mainstream news outlets may peddle false information or that less credible outlets may occasionally break legitimate stories.

ABC News, for example, was forced to suspend a reporter at the end of 2017 for erroneously reporting that former National Security Advisor Michael Flynn would testify that Trump had ordered him to collude with the Russians during the presidential campaign (Wang, 2017). Conversely, the *National Enquirer*, a tabloid typically focused on celebrity gossip and alien sightings, was the first outlet to break the story of the extramarital affair that ended the political career of John Edwards, the 2004 Democratic vice-presidential candidate (Clifford, 2010).

Although these examples are exceptions to the rule, they serve as reminders that blanket approaches to identifying fake news are limited in their usefulness. There is no way to chart every possible venue from which students may access political information, and much of the political information they encounter comes from sources that may not be affiliated with a specific organization. Moreover, even when individuals are presented with evidence that a news source may regularly present misinformation, they may choose to still frequent that source because it speaks to a worldview, and likely a community, with which they identify. The goal for educators, then, should be to have students understand why actual fake news exists, why it is effective in swaying political opinion, and how they can avoid succumbing to it.

PURPOSE AND STRUCTURE OF THE BOOK

Writing a little over six months into the Trump presidency, conservative pundit and frequent critic of the president, Charles Krauthammer (2017), argued that the "guardrails of democracy" were holding despite the chaos that Trump had brought to the White House. Nearly two years into his term, the guardrails are still holding, but one could argue that cracks are beginning to show. Not only has Trump reduced public confidence in the mainstream media, but he and his surrogates have also demonstrated a blatant disregard for verifiable truths, even introducing the phrase "alternative facts" into the cultural lexicon (Dale, 2018; Leonhardt, Philbrick, & Thompson, 2017; NBC News, 2017; Politifact, 2018).

In addition, we have fringe media outlets that have admitted to producing dishonest stories to advance certain narratives and political agendas

(Friedersdorf, 2017). Such outlets are gaining popularity, and social media allows them to reach new readers more easily than ever before. Moreover, recent research by the University of California–Los Angeles's Institute for Democracy, Education, and Access (Rogers et al., 2017) has found that students are increasingly coming to their classes armed with fraudulent information they have encountered online, partially fueling the incivility in schools documented in the aftermath of the 2016 election. Again, the notion of using misinformation for political gain is not an idea that started with Trump; politicians have been lying to hold power and push agendas since antiquity (Carson, 2018). However, the means for disseminating misinformation are more efficient than ever before, creating the need for increased attention to this problem.

This book seeks to move beyond looking at the issue of fake news from a media literacy standpoint. Although media literacy strategies are important, to truly combat the potential civic ramifications of fake news, both educators and students need to understand why fake news works, particularly in an era defined by social media, and how easy it is for even the most astute consumers of political media to succumb to it. For media literacy strategies to have a significant impact on students' practices, educators must first make them aware of systemic issues that allow for the widespread dissemination and consumption of fake news in contemporary society. Classrooms are an ideal space for this type of learning to occur, particularly if one takes the Deweyan view of schools as laboratories for democracy in which students learn to experience aspects of democratic life (Dewey, 1916, 1938).

The book begins by addressing the overarching question of why fake news is effective. In Chapter 1, H. James Garrett provides the theoretical underpinnings that guide the subsequent chapters. He takes a psychosocial lens to the issue of fake news, making the connection between misinformation and individuals' desire to consume information that adheres to their preexisting worldviews. Drawing from political psychology and psychosocial research, Garrett explains how, for many people, reality becomes inseparable from their desire for the world to be a certain way, and thus the desired world becomes their reality of how things are.

Yet, as Garrett notes, the issue of fake news is not new. In Chapter 2, Ashley N. Woodson, LaGarrett J. King, and Esther Kim provide a historical examination of fake news, with a specific focus on how fake news has often served to further marginalize people of color in the United States. From the ways in which news of the Emancipation Proclamation was kept from Black people in the U.S. South during the Civil War to ways the Black Lives Matter movement has been manipulated on social media, their chapter provides a historical context that is needed to understand this contemporary phenomenon.

Although instances of fake news can be found throughout history, the means for disseminating misinformation have become more advanced. In Chapter 3, Ellen Middaugh discusses social media's role in the prevalence of fake news, specifically with respect to how teenagers interact with social media on a daily basis. She uses adolescent development research to explain how adolescents are particularly susceptible to fake news, but she also concludes that these same developmental attributes may allow for opportunities for adolescents to develop the skills and dispositions needed to combat the effects of fake news.

The next two chapters present research detailing the extent to which young people have difficulty discerning fake and biased information online and how those poor reasoning skills impact classroom discussions of political issues. In Chapter 4, Sarah McGrew, Joel Breakstone, Teresa Ortega, Mark Smith, and Sam Wineburg of the Stanford History Education Group present findings from their study of civic online reasoning in which they assessed thousands of students across the United States. From middle school students to college undergraduates in a variety of contexts, students struggled to evaluate online sources—failing to distinguish between news stories and advertisements, verify legitimate social media accounts, and recognize inherent biases within political information found online.

In Chapter 5, Avner Segall, Margaret Crocco, Anne-Lise Halvorsen, and Rebecca Jacobsen illustrate how this failure to recognize misinformation affects students' civic education experiences. They provide excerpts from a high school deliberation on U.S. immigration policy that highlight the ways in which fake news, confirmation bias, and motivated reasoning impacted both the tenor and substance of the discussion. In general, students were not interested in facts that might have challenged their worldview, and many used incorrect, biased, or incomplete information to support their positions on immigration policy.

The final three chapters discuss practical ways K–12 teachers can address elements of fake news in their classes. In Chapter 6, Erica Hodgin and Joseph Kahne offer three approaches to civic media literacy education that help students understand the relationship between digital media and fake news. They encourage helping students develop metacognition related to judging the accuracy and credibility of online information and then providing them with the skills needed to make those judgments. Finally, they argue that providing students with space to practice those skills instills habits that will transfer beyond the classroom setting.

In Chapter 7, Wayne Journell and Christopher H. Clark focus specifically on political memes. These images that convey simple (and often inaccurate) political messages have become ubiquitous on social media, and they pose a unique problem for civic educators. This chapter provides a historical context of the development of political memes, explains why they are an effective form of political persuasion, and offers suggestions for how teachers might effectively broach the subject of political memes in their classes.

Finally, most of the research and theory on addressing fake news in K–12 classrooms has been situated at the secondary level. By that time, however, it may be too late; students need to develop the habits of questioning sources and thinking critically about information at an early age. In Chapter 8, Jennifer Hauver shares eight minilessons that she developed for elementary and middle school students and has implemented in classrooms in Georgia and Virginia. These lessons encourage students to become critical consumers of text, which will help them become critical consumers of political media as they grow older.

Taken collectively, these chapters address the issue of fake news in a way that gets at the roots of the problem. A simple solution to helping students understand and dismiss fake news does not exist, and engaging in this type of instruction will likely be challenging due to the current social context. Yet if educators can move beyond a reactionary approach to fake news and instead help their students understand why fake news is effective, why it is problematic, and how they are culpable in its dissemination, then we may have a shot at limiting its effects in the future. It is worth the try; the future of our democracy is at stake.

NOTE

1. This introduction builds upon recent invited publications on fake news and teaching civics in the Trump era (Journell, 2017, 2018).

REFERENCES

Arceneaux, K., Johnson, M., & Murphy, C. (2012). Polarized political communication, oppositional media hostility, and selective exposure. *Journal of Politics, 74*, 174–186.

Barthell, M., & Mitchell, A. (2017, May 10). Americans' attitudes about the news media deeply divided along partisan lines. *Pew Research Center.* Retrieved from www.journalism.org/2017/05/10/americans-attitudes-about-the-news-media-deeply-divided-along-partisan-lines/

Blake, A. (2018, July 13). Trump denies he said something that he said on a tape everyone has heard. *The Washington Post.* Retrieved from www.washingtonpost.com/news/the-fix/wp/2018/07/13/trump-denies-he-said-something-that-he-said-on-a-tape-that-everyone-has-heard/?utm_term=.4afa652f3191

Borchers, C. (2018, June 18). How images of separated children are shaping the immigration debate. *The Washington Post.* Retrieved from www.washingtonpost.com/news/the-fix/wp/2018/06/18/how-images-of-separated-children-are-shaping-the-immigration-debate/?noredirect=on&utm_term=.14b09edf5471

Bradner, E. (2015, December 2). Trump praises 9/11 truther's 'amazing' reputation. *CNN.* Retrieved from www.cnn.com/2015/12/02/politics/donald-trump-praises-9-11-truther-alex-jones/index.html

Carson, J. (2018, November 28). Fake news: What exactly is it—and how can you spot it? *The Telegraph*. Retrieved from www.telegraph.co.uk/technology/0/fake-news-exactly-has-really-had-influence/

Clifford, S. (2010, March 7). The National Enquirer earns some respect. *The New York Times*. Retrieved from www.nytimes.com/2010/03/08/business/media/08enquirer.html

Cohen, P. (2017, December 20). In tax overhaul, Trump tries to defy the economic odds. *The New York Times*. Retrieved from www.nytimes.com/2017/12/20/business/economy/tax-bill-economy.html?rref=collection%2Fnewseventcollection%2Ftrump-tax-cut-plan&action=click&contentCollection=politics®ion=stream&module=stream_unit&version=latest&contentPlacement=9&pgtype=collection

Coll, S. (2017, December 11). Donald Trump's "fake news" tactics. *The New Yorker*. Retrieved from www.newyorker.com/magazine/2017/12/11/donald-trumps-fake-news-tactics

Concha, J. (2017a, February 23). New York Times launches major ad campaign: 'The truth.' *The Hill*. Retrieved from thehill.com/media/320787-new-york-times-launches-major-ad-campaign-the-truth

Concha, J. (2017b, February 22). The Washington Post: 'Democracy dies in darkness'. *The Hill*. Retrieved from thehill.com/homenews/media/320619-the-washington-post-democracy-dies-in-darkness

Croucher, S. (2018, July 13). Donald Trump calls his own *Sun* interview fake news. *Newsweek*. Retrieved from www.newsweek.com/donald-trump-calls-his-own-sun-interview-fake-news-1022312

Dale, D. (2018, June 20). Donald Trump has said 1726 false things as U.S. president. *Toronto Star*. Retrieved from projects.thestar.com/donald-trump-fact-check/

Delli Carpini, M. X., & Keeter, S. (1996). *What Americans know about politics and why it matters*. New Haven, CT: Yale University Press.

Dewey, J. (1916). *Democracy and education*. New York, NY: Free Press.

Dewey, J. (1938). *Experience and education*. New York, NY: Touchstone.

Drobnic Holan, A., & Sherman, A. (2012, September 24). Barack Obama said 'Fast and Furious' began under the Bush administration. *Politifact*. Retrieved from www.politifact.com/florida/statements/2012/sep/24/barack-obama/barack-obama-said-fast-and-furious-began-under-bus/

Dunn, T. N. (2018, July 13). Trump's Brexit blast: Donald Trump told Theresa May how to do Brexit 'but she wrecked it'—and says the U.S. trade deal is off. *The Sun*. Retrieved from www.thesun.co.uk/news/6766531/trump-may-brexit-us-deal-off/

The Economist. (2017, August 3). Most Republicans trust the president more than they trust the media. In *The Economist* [Website]. Retrieved from www.economist.com/news/united-states/21725822-there-also-broad-support-shutting-down-outlets-perceived-biased-most-republicans

Fischer-Baum, R., Soffen, K., & Long, H. (2018, January 30). Republicans say it's a tax cut for the middle class. The biggest winners are the rich. *The Washington Post*. Retrieved from www.washingtonpost.com/graphics/2017/business/what-republican-tax-plans-could-mean-for-you/?utm_term=.9d83b43e62f1

Friedersdorf, C. (2017, December 29). *Breitbart*'s astonishing confession. *The Atlantic*. Retrieved from www.theatlantic.com/politics/archive/2017/12/the-ongoing-mistreatment-of-right-leaning-news-consumers/549335/

Friedman, U. (2017, December 23). The real-world consequences of 'fake news.' *The Atlantic*. Retrieved from www.theatlantic.com/international/archive/2017/12/trump-world-fake-news/548888/

Giaritelli, A. (2017, December 20). Trump: 'Fake news is working overtime' to 'demean' tax reform bill. *Washington Examiner*. Retrieved from www.washingtonexaminer.com/trump-fake-news-is-working-overtime-to-demean-tax-reform-bill/article/2644005

Gingrich, N. (2017, December 15). Newt Gingrich: Republican tax cuts are hit with fake news attacks. *Fox News*. Retrieved from www.foxnews.com/opinion/2017/12/15/newt-gingrich-republican-tax-cuts-are-hit-with-fake-news-attacks.html

Graves, L. (2017, August 17). This is Sinclair, 'the most dangerous US company you've never heard of'. *The Guardian*. Retrieved from www.theguardian.com/media/2017/aug/17/sinclair-news-media-fox-trump-white-house-circa-breitbart-news

Guess, A., Nyhan, B., & Reifler, J. (2017). *"You're fake news!": Findings from the Poynter media trust survey*. St. Petersburg, FL: The Poynter Institute. Retrieved from poyntercdn.blob.core.windows.net/files/PoynterMediaTrustSurvey2017.pdf

Gunther, A. C. (1992). Biased press or biased public? Attitudes toward media coverage of social groups. *Public Opinion Quarterly, 56*, 147–167.

Gutmann, A., & Thompson, D. (2004). *Why deliberative democracy?* Princeton, NJ: Princeton University Press.

Habermas, J. (1984). *The theory of communicative action: Volume 1: Reason and the rationalization of society* (T. McCarthy, Trans.). Boston, MA: Beacon. (Original work published 1981)

Habermas, J. (1989). *The structural transformation of the public sphere: An inquiry into a category of bourgeois society* (T. Burger & F. Lawrence, Trans.). Cambridge, MA: MIT Press. (Original work published 1962)

Hanna, J. (2017, January 27). What is Infowars? *CNN*. Retrieved from www.cnn.com/2017/01/27/politics/infowars-explainer/index.html

Heafner, T. L., Triplett, N., Handler, L., & Massey, D. (2018). Situated word learning: Words of the year (WsOY) and social studies inquiry. *Theory & Research in Social Education, 46*, 110–148.

Hess, D. E., & McAvoy, P. (2015). *The political classroom: Evidence and ethics in democratic education*. New York, NY: Routledge.

Hochschild, J. L., & Einstein, K. L. (2015). *Do facts matter? Information and misinformation in American politics*. Norman: University of Oklahoma Press.

Isaac, M., & Wakabayashi, D. (2017, October 30). Russian influence reached 126 million through Facebook alone. *The New York Times*. Retrieved from www.nytimes.com/2017/10/30/technology/facebook-google-russia.html

Journell, W. (2017). Fake news, alternative facts, and Trump: Teaching social studies in a post-truth era. *Social Studies Journal, 37*(1), 8–21.

Journell, W. (2018). Civic education in a post-truth society: Combating "fake news" and "alternative facts." In J. Clabough & T. Lintner (Eds.), *No reluctant citizens: Teaching civics in K–12 classrooms* (pp. 113–129). Charlotte, NC: Information Age.

Krauthammer, C. (2017, August 3). The guardrails hold. *The Washington Post.* Retrieved from www.washingtonpost.com/opinions/the-guardrails-hold/2017/08/03/fcfc157c-7877-11e7-9eac-d56bd5568db8_story.html?utm_term=.459fcbf1840a

Kudlow, L. (2017, December 2). I'd vote for it. You should, too. *National Review.* Retrieved from www.nationalreview.com/article/454294/congressional-tax-cut-plan-will-spark-investment-boom-and-rapid-economic-growth-will

Lee, T.-T. (2005). The liberal media myth revisited: An examination of factors influencing perceptions of media bias. *Journal of Broadcasting & Electronic Media, 49,* 43-64.

Leonhardt, D., Philbrick, I. P., & Thompson, S. A. (2017, December 14). Trump's lies vs. Obama's. *The New York Times.* Retrieved from www.nytimes.com/interactive/2017/12/14/opinion/sunday/trump-lies-obama-who-is-worse.html

Lima, C. (2018, January 18). HuffPost shutters unpaid contributor platform. *Politico.* Retrieved from www.politico.com/story/2018/01/18/huffpost-no-unpaid-contributors-345535

Madsen, W. (2016, February 25). Why Scalia's death suggests cover-up. *InfoWars.* Retrieved from www.infowars.com/why-scalias-death-suggests-cover-up/

Mill, J. S. (1975). *On liberty.* New York, NY: Norton. (Original work published 1859)

Moore, S. (2017, December 3). Tax cut for everyone. *The Washington Times.* Retrieved from www.washingtontimes.com/news/2017/dec/3/tax-plan-is-a-cut-for-everyone/

NBC News. (2017, January 22). Meet the Press 01/22/17. Retrieved from www.nbcnews.com/meet-the-press/meet-press-01-22-17-n710491

North Idaho College. (2018). Information skills—fake news. In *Molstead Library Research Guides.* Retrieved from nic.libguides.com/evalnews

Politifact. (2018, January 3). Donald Trump's file. Retrieved from www.politifact.com/personalities/donald-trump/

Quigley, A. (2017, June 16). Who is Alex Jones? His top five conspiracy theories ahead of NBC's Megyn Kelly interview. *Newsweek.* Retrieved from www.newsweek.com/who-alex-jones-his-top-five-conspiracy-theories-ahead-nbc-megyn-kelly-626633

Rawls, J. (1993). *Political liberalism.* New York, NY: Columbia University Press.

Rogers, J., Franke, M., Yun, J.-E. E., Ishimoto, M., Diera, C., Geller, R. C., . . . Brenes, T. (2017). *Teaching and learning in the age of Trump: Increasing stress and hostility in America's high schools.* Los Angeles, CA: University of California–Los Angeles Institute for Democracy, Education, and Access.

Rutenberg, J. (2017, February 19). In Trump's volleys, echoes of Alex Jones's conspiracy theories. *The New York Times.* Retrieved from www.nytimes.com/2017/02/19/business/media/alex-jones-conspiracy-theories-donald-trump.html

Savransky, R. (2016, October 17). Trump retweets top InfoWars editor. *The Hill.* Retrieved from thehill.com/blogs/ballot-box/presidential-races/301298-trump-retweets-top-infowars-editor-one-day-after-clinton

Schudson, M. (1978). *Discovering the news: A social history of American newspapers.* New York, NY: Basic Books.

Shapiro, L. (2017, November 1). Anatomy of a Russian Facebook ad. *The*

Washington Post. Retrieved from www.washingtonpost.com/graphics/2017/business/russian-ads-facebook-anatomy/?utm_term=.b02bf396f38d

Southern Poverty Law Center. (2018). Alex Jones. Retrieved from www.splcenter.org/fighting-hate/extremist-files/individual/alex-jones

Swift, A. (2016, September 14). Americans' trust in mass media sinks to new low. *Gallup News*. Retrieved from news.gallup.com/poll/195542/americans-trust-mass-media-sinks-new-low.aspx

Wang, V. (2017, December 2). ABC suspends reporter Brian Ross over erroneous report about Trump. *The New York Times*. Retrieved from www.nytimes.com/2017/12/02/us/brian-ross-suspended-abc.html

The Washington Post. (2017). The intelligence community report on Russian activities in the 2016 election. In *The Washington Post* [Website]. Retrieved from www.washingtonpost.com/apps/g/page/politics/the-intelligence-community-report-on-russian-activities-in-the-2016-election/2153/

CHAPTER 1

Why Does Fake News Work?

On the Psychosocial Dynamics of Learning, Belief, and Citizenship

H. James Garrett

The fake news phenomenon puts a localized pressure on K–12 educators. In light of this pressure, as well as the position of fake news in a complex media ecology, there is currently an urgent need to conceptualize this phenomenon and develop pedagogical interventions. Young people need to be introduced to practices that build their capacity to understand the sociopolitical world around them, and that capacity now includes an understanding of fake news.

This chapter, however, is not necessarily concerned with those practices. Rather, the purpose of this chapter is to elaborate on the contours of the fake news phenomenon, including a closer look at what the phrase signifies, before moving to a psychosocial accounting for why and how fake news seems to function. The question to which I return throughout the chapter is: Why does fake news work?

Fake news is located in an ecology of tribal partisanship, media proliferation, media fragmentation, and a civic education[1] lacking in pedagogies addressing media literacy. Fake news is simultaneously nothing new and novel. It is both a concrete unjustifiable thing and an ephemeral invocation of doubt.

Fake news operates through sophisticated microtargeting practices predicated upon analysis of metadata and created for the nefarious purposes of further calcifying partisan division. Fake news works because of the ways that media literacy and civic education are underattended and undervalued in K–12 formal schooling. Fake news functions by hitting particular veins of desire, identification, defense, and emotional investment. Without an understanding of each of the difficult facets of fake news and the broader ecology in which it exists, any pedagogical interventions are likely to treat the symptoms but ignore the cause.

This chapter is meant to address fake news in a way that forwards interpretations of just how destabilizing and worrying it is, but also to offer reasons why it seems to be taking such a tight hold in our sociopolitical present. I will begin by forwarding a taxonomy of fake news that involves three overlapping phenomena:

- A historical precedent
- A current reality
- An invective used to instill doubt and mistrust

I will then elaborate on the emotional or affective processes identified by political psychologists, called "motivated reasoning" and "cognitive bias," into which fake news plays. Finally, I will offer psychodynamic accounts of how fantasy, affect, fear, and desire also play significant roles in the ways in which fake news operates in and out of classrooms.

A TAXONOMY OF FAKE NEWS

The first consideration when thinking about fake news is the imprecision with which the term functions and circulates. Because it can mean so many things, and because it has risen to such prominence as a phrase in the last few years, the phrase can be uttered with nods of agreement but without an agreed-upon definition. Fake news can signify at least three different types of phenomena, each well-functioning in our current sociopolitical landscape, each housing more fine-grained distinctions, and each overlapping with the others:

- An implausible and false story
- A plausible, though fabricated, story that is disseminated through social media using sophisticated targeting strategies
- A dismissive phrase used to sow doubt and uncertainty onto an account of a situation about which the user of the phrase disagrees

Fake News as Tabloid Un-Truths

The first phenomenon consists of implausible and false stories, often sensationalized stories that are conjured up for entertainment purposes. Tabloid outlets, while from time to time landing on a veracious story, have historically disseminated this kind of fake news. These are the stories of alien landings and demonic possessions, accounts of celebrity indiscretion, and reports of political scandal. The purpose of this sort of fake news is, broadly, entertainment. They are, literally, fake news stories in that they conjure fiction and are presented in the form or genre of news. This kind of fake news story is relatively easy to dismiss. It is also the simplest to understand.

Satire and parody also fall under this type of fake news. *The Daily Show*, *The Onion*, *Saturday Night Live*, and other outlets have existed for decades and have posed, in some form or fashion, as "news" but are, by definition, fake. The purpose of this sort of fake news is either to make light of a particular political issue or to use humor in order to point out a contradiction or a tension and offer a form of cultural critique (Garrett & Schmeichel, 2012; Garrett & Segall, 2015). This type of fake news works as a function of the cultural milieu and a desire for distraction and/or cultural critique.

Fake News as Targeted Disinformation

The second phenomenon is the kind of fake news that is currently receiving the most attention in media and pedagogy circles. This type of fake news rose to notoriety during the 2016 presidential election, though it was on the radar as a phrase as early as 2014. Much has been made of the fake news that was generated by entities around the world and circulated through Facebook, Twitter, and other social media outlets. This type of fake news closely resembles traditional types of "disinformation," as it functions in a targeted way to shape people's beliefs and actions in the political arena. In other words, this kind of fake news is targeted, directed, and motivated by investments in partisan outcomes.

Like the first manifestation of fake news where conjured stories have been around for some time, disinformation is nothing new either. For most of the 20th century, as mass communications developed and spread, disinformation was spread by nation-states and recognized as propaganda (Carson, 2018). This sort of fake news circulates for the purposes of currying favor for a particular point of view, and it functions on the premises of persuasion. The sort of fake news that is getting the most attention now has its roots here, but it has been accelerated and complicated by social media networks.

This distinction is where fake news gets complicated. Elements of these first two types of fake news phenomena are present (entertainment and party-sponsored disinformation or propaganda), but then the factors of "big data," social media, Web 2.0 user-generated platforms, and the democratization of digital participation are added. Here is where we see the generation of misinformation being motivated not only by power and influence, but also by advertisement revenue and profit. In short, fake news is a business model (Sydell, 2016).

Facebook, for example, was, and remains, a key location in the fake news ecology due to the use of its data, audience, and reach during the 2016 campaign. Facebook is a location for all of the types of fake news already discussed. There are the traditional "fake" stories, satire, disinformation, and propaganda from official campaigns, but then we add targeted campaigns by foreign governments to incite division, sow distrust, and profit-motivated purveyors of fake content without any partisan motivation whatsoever.

So, while critiquing Facebook as a place from which to retrieve news seems a legitimate starting point, educators may also need to think about parsing the layers of fake news as well. Perhaps we could consider learning from Facebook itself, as its research team reported on the need for more specific language about fake news from within that corporation:

> The term "fake news" has emerged as a catch-all phrase to refer to everything from news articles that are factually incorrect to opinion pieces, parodies and sarcasm, hoaxes, rumors, memes, online abuse, and factual misstatements by public figures that are reported in otherwise accurate news pieces. The overuse and misuse of the term "fake news" can be problematic because, without common definitions, we cannot understand or fully address these issues. (Wheedon, Nuland, & Stamos, 2017, p. 4)

For the authors of that report, then, this second "fake news" phenomenon is more complicated than the first because it reveals other phenomena: what they call information operations, false news, false amplifiers, and disinformation. Those phenomena are interrelated and exist in relation to one another but nonetheless point to the necessity of distinguishing between various types of misinformation.

This type of fake news works not just because teenagers in other countries make up false stories and post them online, but also because of the sophisticated data-informed targeting practices that allow those stories to circulate and thus provide advertisement revenue. While this kind of fake news works because of the sophisticated targeting, coordination, and use of big data, it also works because of an exploitation of desire and identification.

Fake News as a Weaponized Phrase

The third fake news phenomenon is its use as a phrase to dismiss otherwise credible news reports as false. It draws upon the emergence of the second type, which is the premise upon which it is used, but it is used to deflect unwanted attention by dismissing it as "fake." For example, President Trump began using this phrase as a derisive charge toward reporters and accounts of incidents that cut against his interests. Its use in this way is meant to introduce and maintain doubt into the public conversation, as legitimate sources and reports of events are said by "the most powerful person in the world" to be, in his words, "fake" or "false."

This type of fake news may seem simple and be dismissed as just a person lying for personal and political gain. However, considering this phenomenon as simple is dangerous. What Trump and others are doing is complicated. They are, indeed, playing upon underlying and ongoing fissures and frictions existing in our political discourse.

Yet these strategies only work within a context that allows them to flow. News media outlets cover Trump's tweets, providing access to them to millions of additional readers/viewers. It is cheaper to have commentators ruminating over Trump's latest tweets than it is to produce in-depth journalism about the substantive issues of the day (Riley-Smith, 2018).

Three Types of Fake News and Education

To underscore, fake news does not work simply because someone articulates or writes an inaccurate story. There have to be structures in place for them to circulate and audiences to view or click them. There has to be a genre that preexists the article or utterance into which it can be understood and loved or hated. Fake news works because there is more to it than reading news for truth or fiction.

For example, if we are thinking about social media, it is, of course, crucial to help students identify the fake from the reputable. Yet even this approach avoids a more crucial issue, that of the degree to which users of social media sites (Facebook, Instagram, and so on) are a product, not the consumer. The consumers, the customers, are the agencies and business that buy advertisements, in essence paying for our eyes and clicks. Our interests are monetized, and because social media is a multibillion-dollar business model, there is no clear incentive for Facebook or Twitter to fix this problem.

So what is the answer? In our capacity as educators, there ought to be some curricular thought and attention given to developing knowledge about how social media works. Part of it is the business model, and another significant part of it resides within us, in our interest and investments in both creating and viewing content. In other words, fake news works because it makes people money; and fake news works because we like it.

My point here is that there is something at stake in making sure that pedagogical structures are present to help students understand that President Trump's rhetoric is dangerous, but also that the danger only has potency because of the ecology of the sociopolitical landscape into which it is introduced. It is not untrue, for example, that particular media outlets on the right *and* the left work to further particular partisan narratives. This partisan divide makes charges of fake news so effective because the audience can confirm their already existing beliefs by finding similarly partisan narratives to reinforce this view. It is the relationship between belief, personal investments, and nonrational processes to which I turn in the next section.

POLITICAL PSYCHOLOGY, PSYCHOSOCIAL THEORIES, AND THE PRESSING NEED FOR EMOTIONAL CONCEPTUALIZATIONS IN EDUCATION

The types of fake news phenomena discussed above overlap and intersect, and the result is that we have quite the mess. However, the reason why fake news functions is not only because of a lack of ability to parse fact from fiction or bias from objectivity, but it also has to do with the psychosocial elements of individuals and groups of citizens who encounter political information through a circuitry that goes beyond rational analysis. In the remainder of this chapter, I explore different ways of interpreting these areas beyond rationality from the perspectives of political psychology, psychosocial studies, and psychoanalysis.

Motivated Reasoning, Confirmation Bias, and the Backfire Effect

Over the past two decades or so, several terms have emerged from political psychology and sociology that point to nonrational, emotional, and affective processes that are part and parcel of our political thinking apparatus. Motivated reasoning, confirmation bias, and the backfire effect each locate and describe ways in which encountering political information enlivens our emotional circuitry.

Motivated reasoning is a term of engagement signifying how individuals interpret newly encountered information in ways that advantage their already-held views. Motivated reasoning points to a process where "once people have developed a worldview . . . they are extremely resistant to information that would require them to change that worldview" (Dusso & Kennedy, 2015, p. 62). People are not, researchers find, considering what they see on the news as functions of multiple perspectives used to update their understanding of current political issues. Rather, information that bolsters their view is accommodated and that which challenges it is dismissed.

In most cases, people are not conscious of this process. In other words, it is not done intentionally. Political scientists Charles Taber and Milton Lodge (2016) noted that the processes involved in motivated reasoning "are often unnoticed forces and processes that occur in the early, unconscious phases of information processing" (p. 62).

While many people prefer to view themselves as rational interpreters of information, Taber and Lodge (2016) explain that "our explicit reasoning processes serve to *rationalize* behavior rather than to cause it" (p. 62). Their studies have demonstrated that what we understand as dispassionate analysis covers over more invisible ways in which our individual histories and ways of knowing influence interpretation.

Another term emanating from political psychology is *confirmation bias*, and it similarly points to the processes by which individuals are biased toward "seeking or interpreting of evidence in ways that are partial to existing beliefs, expectations, or a hypothesis at hand" (Nickerson, 1998, p. 175). A significant feature of confirmation bias, just like motivated reasoning, is the recognition by researchers that it occurs unwittingly.

Thus a worrying trend identified in political science and political psychology is even when errata are reported and corrections offered to mistaken reports, the mistaken reports persist in the consciousness of those who believed them to begin with. One prominent example of this phenomenon is the persistence of belief that Saddam Hussein was hiding stockpiles of weapons of mass destruction in Iraq in the early part of the 2000s. Despite objective proof to the contrary, that belief still persists.

In fact, for some people, there is yet another process at play called the *backfire effect* in which people dismiss information and evidence that runs contrary to their prior beliefs and their prior beliefs get stronger. Political scientists Brendan Nyhan and Jason Reifler's (2010) work on the backfire effect has garnered a great deal of attention in the public discourse around political understanding and decision making. This backfire effect runs counterintuitively to commonsense notions of learning that hold that when learners find new evidence, they will update their views to accommodate that new evidence.

What political scientists are finding is that there are more processes at play than simply adding information to our understanding. There are emotional and affective aspects of our learning about the sociopolitical world. These processes are also reasons why fake news works. The reports, while false or misleading, fit into preexisting worldviews and take advantage of our disposition to believe what is comforting.

However, this sort of intellectual process is not exclusive to political reasoning. Education researchers, for example, can deliver mountains of evidence regarding the rich teaching practices that most benefit students, yet legislators ignore it in favor of more politically expedient rules. Climate researchers persistently see their studies presented as "controversial" despite the near unanimous consensus within the scientific community surrounding the issue of global warming (Oreskes & Conway, 2011). Comprehensive sex education has been shown to correlate with reduction in unwanted pregnancy and sexually transmitted infections, yet abstinence-only programs persist. The problem, as these studies show, is not the lack of good information. Instead, the problem is located in the moments of encounter and interpretation.

Motivated Reasoning, Fake News, and K–12 Education

What this information means for K–12 education is that there are problems not just about the ways in which educators can aid students' acquisition of knowledge, but also about how they encounter that knowledge in the first place. Within civic education, much of the focus on deliberation, discussion, and engagement with current issues relies on a building up of our rational capacity to engage in dialogue.

For example, Sarah McGrew, Joel Breakstone, Theresa Ortega, Mark Smith, and Sam Wineburg (2018) of the Stanford History Education Group have provided invaluable insight into the challenges that educators face. In their work, they found that "students struggle to engage in even basic evaluations" of online sources (p. 187) and have suggested structured support for students' practice in developing analytic skills.

Social studies scholar Wayne Journell (2017) has suggested assigning the role of "fact-checker" for students to take as they develop such skills, a strategy that has shown pedagogical potential. There is no doubt that these are important skills to develop as young people enter the official political arena and begin to take part in the legislative and governing processes through their participation (or lack thereof).

Educators are taking note, however, of motivated reasoning and cognitive bias (Clark & Avery, 2016; Journell, 2017). For example, civic educators Joseph Kahne and Benjamin Bowyer (2017) identified motivated reasoning as a problem for civic education and have studied its presence in educational contexts. They recognized the complex media and information ecology in which information circulates, and ultimately concluded that youth were more likely to judge something as accurate when it aligned with prior partisan views.

Social studies educators Margaret Crocco, Anne-Lise Halvorsen, Rebecca Jacobsen, and Avner Segall (2018), in their investigations of social studies students' use of evidence in making arguments, found that "despite being given carefully curated evidence packets, students tended to dismiss this evidence in favor of outside sources" (p. 68). Indeed, the students used classroom deliberations in order to justify their previously held views, a process that corroborates the findings of the political psychologists who study motivated reasoning.

In their exploration of motivated reasoning in civic education, Kahne and Bowyer (2017) presented counterintuitive findings, such as the way in which more content knowledge correlates with higher degrees of partisanship and ideological rigidity. As it turns out, then, the more one knows may not necessarily lead to more informed decisions, given that "the biases associated with [motivated] reasoning are greatest among those with the most political knowledge" (p. 7). Such a result corroborates political scientists Aaron Dusso and Sheila Kennedy's (2015) finding that "education or increased political interest and awareness are not enough to defeat the pernicious effects of a highly-polarized political system" (p. 60).

However, not all of the research paints such a dire picture. There are places where educators and researchers can intervene. Kahne and Bowyer

(2017) presented a finding, for example, that students with formal media literacy education were better able to navigate information and were less prone to biased interpretations.

Further, while Nyhan and Reifler's (2010) dissemination of the backfire effect has alarmed psychologists, policymakers, and educators, political scientists Thomas Wood and Ethan Porter (2018) have begun to challenge the backfire effect in showing that people are indeed able to accommodate facts and change their minds in accordance with them.

Marshall Alcorn (2013), a faculty member at the Washington Center of Psychoanalysis, has elaborated on the processes by which people, when primed by being asked to remember a time during which they were successful at something, were much more open to new and contradicting information. Fake news works, at least in part, because the kinds of stories circulating under that signifier seem to "fit" into our already existing worldviews

UNDERSTANDING FAKE NEWS AS A PSYCHOSOCIAL PHENOMENON

In this section I conceptualize fake news as not only a problem that exists "out there," as big data informs the targeting decisions of operatives bent on instigating and deepening already existing political divides. The problem of fake news is also "in here," in the messages that circulate, find purchase, and resonate within us. The messages we see become tied up with our wishes and desires about what we want (and what we want to avoid) in or from the world. Fake news works, in this sense, because of the ways that it comes with a set of feelings; it plays on our desires, fears, wishes, and fantasies.

In other words, and in light of the above section about motivated reasoning, unconscious processes can be considered an underattended feature of the circuitry through which fake news operates. I turn now from the language of political psychology to the language of psychoanalysis. From this vantage, when we are engaging in political questions (e.g., what should we do together, as a group, to address the issues we together face?), there are several less-than-rational processes that speak to the emotional, affective, or what we might call "psychosocial" processes.

Psychosocial theories are used to analyze the ways that sociological and political understandings are infused with elements of our personal lives, and vice versa. They explore processes of coming to know the world through the meanings we make therein. Meaning is made not only through the rational analysis of incoming information, but also by the ways in which experience or information mishes and mashes with our own lives, our histories of being with others. Psychosocial researcher Stephen Frosh (2014) has stated that psychosocial studies

> . . . seeks to investigate the ways in which psychic and social processes demand to be understood as always implicated in each other, as mutually constitutive, coproduced, or abstracted levels of a single dialectical process. As such it can be understood as an interdisciplinary field in search of transdisciplinary objects of knowledge. Psychosocial Studies is also distinguished by its emphasis on affect, the irrational and unconscious processes, often, but not necessarily, understood psychoanalytically. (p. 161)

Therefore, thinking psychosocially means that it is a phenomenon that has all of the elements described above but that it also plays on the personal manifestations of meaning making. Fake news, in all of those types outlined above, trades in these histories and the ways in which they introduce new conflicts and enliven old ones.

After all, fake news stories get clicks and views on social media because they offer an invitation, a beckoning, toward some affective state: anger, vindictiveness, relief, or otherwise. Thinking psychosocially provides a way to think about the function of fake news that allows for a focus on those irrational and unconscious processes located by the political psychologists but, importantly, does not disavow the crucial aspects of developing skills in analysis and evidence.

Looking Within

There is much more to "knowing" than whether we do or do not know something. There is the "what" of learning, but there is also the "how" and the ways that what we know attach to our values, personal histories, and emotional investments. At different times, and in different contexts, we seek out information, incorporate, refuse, or dismiss it. We have different reasons for what we call learning. Sometimes we learn something for instrumental reasons like passing a test or finding out how many layers of clothes to wear in light of a weather forecast.

There are other situations, those that cut against deeply held emotional convictions, in which we learn things and refuse to understand them at the same time, what psychoanalysts call resistance (Garrett & Segall, 2013; Pitt, 1998). Sometimes we learn in order to satiate a yearning to know more, borne out of curiosity. Other times, though, we learn so that we can use our knowledge as a weapon.

In this line of thinking, individuals are cautioned to see this process not only playing out in others, but also within themselves. For example, in seeing and critiquing Trump as holding to partial versions of the truth and reveling in his tweets, I (writing autobiographically) am tempted to ignore the ways that my knowledge is also partial. This disposition is not about equivocating (not all partiality is created equally), but it is about understanding the directions and intensities of our attention and critique.

In elaborating this point, psychoanalyst Steven Tublin (2017) wrote about his own political knowledge with self-suspicion and honesty:

> Through a long campaign of vigorous procrastination, I have accumulated a vast storehouse of information about government, political figures, and public policy options. But the truth is, I don't know nearly enough to justify the certainty I have long felt about how to run the country. I have, for instance, strong feelings about the appropriate level of military spending given the current size of the American economy, but in all honesty, I don't really know what we spend the money on or what risks we might face if we, say, halved it. These giant gaps in my understanding tell me that I—along with everyone else—ought to be far less confident about my politics than I am. (p. 512)

What Tublin is articulating is that in all matters where deep convictions are held, we are in the midst of irrational processes of accommodating and dismissing evidence and placing emotional value not only on the information we possess, but also on how it stands in relationship to others and the knowledge that they possess and deploy. In Tublin's writing there is acknowledgement of the facts, but also the notion that those facts are put in the service of something that we would typically call an argument.

What Tublin (2017) acknowledges is that his knowledge is partial, as all of our knowledge must be. He is saying that such partiality is all of our burden to bear and that learning about social and political issues informs us of our own wishes as much as it does about the matters of the day. Therefore, the *manner* of learning and how that comes to have an effect on us, not only as thinkers but also as people who act in the world, is an increasingly important aspect of political thinking and social knowledge. Fake news, then, may work not on *what* we know, but *how* we know it and what we think it means. It also works if we think only "the other side" is susceptible to it.

Magical Thinking and the Weaponization of Fake News

Psychosocial theories suggest that we understand thought as comprised of our rational cognitive abilities, as well as the feelings and affective states that accompany or precede them. In other words, there is never a solely rational moment devoid of affect, feeling, or emotion. However, there is a type of thinking that *is* solely nonrational—what psychoanalyst Thomas Ogden (2010) has called "magical thinking"—and can help offer one final way to understand why fake news works. Magical thinking refers to "thinking that relies on omnipotent fantasy to create a psychic reality the individual experiences as 'more real' than external reality" (p. 319).

In moments of magical thinking, the actual reality of the world is inseparable from the desire for things to be a certain way. The desire for things to be true becomes the reality of how things are. It leads to a situation in which the thinker "treats his thoughts and feeling not as subjective experiences, but as facts" (Ogden, 2010, p. 321). In some of the most alarming uses of the term *fake news*, magical thinking appears an appropriate label.

Fake news works as an invocation of doubt or dismissal of reality and operates on the "illusion that one is not subject to the laws that apply to others" (Ogden, 2010, p. 321). Magical thinking is convenient because it allows the thinker to avoid unpleasant thoughts or the idea that they may be wrong. It is a type of encounter with information that erases the possibility for other people to have their own realities and thus, while convenient, is quite dangerous.

Up to this point, the psychodynamic pushes and pulls of logic and rationalization are, to varying degrees, found on all points of the ideological spectrum. Magical thinking is, however, exhibited squarely in Trump's operational use of the term *fake news*. Our attention to the executive branch and the presidency, therefore, is warranted.

When a powerful leader utilizes the term fake news in that third version in order to dismiss as false an undesirable truth, that leader is leaning on the process of magical thinking in order to forge their own reality. Such a psychodynamic conceptualization corroborates the empirical social science underlying motivated reasoning and confirmation bias. Motivated reasoning works, perhaps, because of an individual tendency toward this kind of magical thinking.

Our urgent concern is appropriate regarding fake news as magical thinking because "it has one overriding drawback: it does not 'work'—nothing can be built on it or with it except layers of magical constructions" (Ogden, 2010, p. 322). What is worrying is that more and more fantasy is built on top of itself, and there seems to be sufficient purchase in the public imaginary in the fantasy itself.

As educators, though, the consequences of governance occurring on the back of magical constructions are dire. Without the recognition of, and ability to contend with, reality, the president and the electorate are operating a high-stakes game without much of a safety net. Fake news works because it allows for a continuation of a dangerous fantasy: that we can live without consequence.

CONCLUSIONS

There is indeed cause for alarm. Fake news works. The more people know, the more likely they are to be deeply partisan rather than open to new ways of thinking (Dusso & Kennedy, 2015; Kahne & Bowyer, 2017). Therefore, we need different narratives than simply "the more you know." Further, as Wineburg, McGrew, Breakstone, and Ortega (2016) of the Stanford History Education Group found, middle school through university students were, by and large, unsophisticated analyzers of online information. They offered a sober conclusion:

> Never have we had so much information at our fingertips. Whether this bounty will make us smarter and better informed or more ignorant and narrow-minded will depend on our awareness of this problem and our educational response to it. At present, we worry that democracy is threatened by the ease at which disinformation is allowed to spread and flourish. (p. 5)

Here again we learn that the problem is not a lack of information or knowledge. What these researchers concluded was that a focus on analysis and argumentation is a necessary component to any appropriate civic education in the 21st century.

I agree. However, what is also needed is a recognition that civic action, political knowledge, and engaged participation are influenced by much more than the ability to evaluate evidence; they are influenced by the psychical investments we have in those issues as well. Political psychologists are corroborating what psychoanalysts have long known: namely that the sense we make of the world is never free from the intimate emotional connections out of which we forge our subjectivity.

Fake news operates on top of these intertwined processes, where they wrap over and onto each other, making one seem almost the same as the other. Fake news works because of the degree to which those producing it are able to capitalize on the affective dimensions of our political thinking apparatus—the motivated reasoning, confirmation bias, and psychical circuitry that defends thinkers from the discomfort inherent in learning that which disquiets. In whatever comes of our pedagogical addressing of the fake news phenomenon, it would seem that part of it needs to be the ways in which our orientation to news is significantly influenced by our emotional attachments and psychical investments in particular stories about the world.

NOTE

1. "Civic education," in this chapter, is conceptualized as that which occurs in formal schooling and through cultural participation.

REFERENCES

Alcorn, M. (2013). *Resistance to learning: Overcoming the desire not to know in classroom teaching*. New York, NY: Palgrave MacMillan.

Carson, J. (2018, November 28). Fake news: What exactly is it—and how can you spot it? *The Telegraph*. Retrieved from www.telegraph.co.uk/technology/0/fake-news-exactly-has-really-had-influence/

Clark, C. H., & Avery, P. G. (2016). The psychology of controversial issues' discussions: Challenges and opportunities in a polarized, post 9/11 society. In W. Journell (Ed.), *Reassessing the social studies curriculum: Promoting critical civic engagement in a politically polarized, post 9/11 world* (pp. 109–120). Lanham, MD: Rowman & Littlefield.

Crocco, M. S., Halvorsen, A.-L., Jacobsen, R. J., & Segall, A. (2018). Less arguing, more listening: Improving civility in classrooms. *Phi Delta Kappan, 99*(5), 67–71.

Dusso, A., & Kennedy, S. S. (2015). Does ignorance matter? The relative importance of civic knowledge and the human tendency to engage in motivated reasoning. *Journal of Public and Nonprofit Affairs, 1*, 59–72.

Frosh, S. (2014). The nature of the psychosocial: Debates from *Studies in the Psychosocial. Journal of Psycho-Social Studies, 8*, 159–169.

Garrett, H. J., & Schmeichel, M. (2012). Using *The Daily Show* to promote media literacy. *Social Education, 76*, 211–215.

Garrett, H. J., & Segall, A. (2013). (Re)considerations of ignorance and resistance in teacher education. *Journal of Teacher Education, 64*, 294–304.

Garrett, H. J., & Segall, A. (2015). Critical race theory, psychoanalysis, and social studies pedagogy. In P. Chandler (Ed.), *Doing race in social studies: Critical perspectives* (pp. 279–296). Charlotte, NC: Information Age.

Journell, W. (2017). Fake news, alternative facts, and Trump: Teaching social studies in a post truth era. *Social Studies Journal, 37*(1), 8–21.

Kahne, J., & Bowyer, B. (2017). Educating for democracy in a partisan age: Confronting the challenges of motivated reasoning and misinformation. *American Educational Research Journal, 54*, 3–34.

McGrew, S., Breakstone, J., Ortega, T., Smith, M., & Wineburg, S. (2018). Can students evaluate online sources? Learning from assessments of civic online reasoning. *Theory & Research in Social Education, 46*, 165–193.

Nickerson, R. S. (1998). Confirmation bias: A ubiquitous phenomenon in many guises. *Review of General Psychology, 2*, 175–220.

Nyhan, B., & Reifler, J. (2010). When corrections fail: The persistence of political misperceptions. *Political Behavior, 32*, 303–330.

Ogden, T. H. (2010). On three forms of thinking: magical thinking, dream thinking, and transformative thinking. *The Psychoanalytic Quarterly, 79*, 317–347.

Oreskes, N., & Conway, E. M. (2011). *Merchants of doubt: How a handful of scientists obscured the truth on issues from tobacco smoke to global warming*. New York, NY: Bloomsbury Press.

Pitt, A. J. (1998). Qualifying resistance: Some comments on methodological dilemmas. *International Journal of Qualitative Studies in Education, 11*, 535–553.

Riley-Smith, B. (2018, January 19). Why Donald Trump's Twitter strategy is more sophisticated than you might think. *The Telegraph*. Retrieved from www.telegraph.co.uk/news/2018/01/19/donald-trumps-twitter-strategy-sophisticated-might-think/

Sydell, L. (2016, November 23). We tracked down a fake-news creator in the suburbs. Here's what we learned. *NPR, All Tech Considered* [Heard on *All Things Considered*]. Retrieved from www.npr.org/sections/

alltechconsidered/2016/11/23/503146770/npr-finds-the-head-of-a-covert-fake-news-operation-in-the-suburbs

Taber, C. S., & Lodge, M. (2016). The illusion of choice in democratic politics: The unconscious impact of motivated political reasoning. *Advances in Political Psychology, 37*, 61–85.

Tublin, S. (2017) Partisanship in the psychoanalytic community: Navigating the conflicting roles of citizen and analyst amid Trump-era polarization. *Contemporary Psychoanalysis, 53*, 505–515.

Wheedon, J., Nuland, W., & Stamos, A. (2017). Information operations and Facebook. *Facebook Security.* Retrieved from fbnewsroomus.files.wordpress.com/2017/04/facebook-and-information-operations-v1.pdf

Wineburg, S., McGrew, S., Breakstone, J., & Ortega, T. (2016). *Evaluating information: The cornerstone of civic online reasoning*. Stanford, CA: Stanford University Digital Repository. Retrieved from purl.stanford.edu/fv751yt5934

Wood, T., & Porter, E. (2018). The elusive backfire effect: Mass attitudes' steadfast factual adherence. *Political Behavior*. Advance online publication. doi: 10.1007/s11109-018-9443-y

CHAPTER 2

Real Recognize Real

Thoughts on Race, Fake News, and Naming Our Truths

Ashley N. Woodson, LaGarrett J. King, and Esther Kim

Most who have written on the issue argue that fake news is bad because it is a threat to informed citizenry in an aspiring democracy (e.g., Allcot & Gentzkow, 2017). We generally agree. However, this fact alone would not justify the growing public obsession with fake news. For example, capitalism is also a threat to informed citizenry in an aspiring democracy, and relatively few people seem genuinely worried about that.

It would also be difficult to argue that the fakeness of fake news is uniquely or inherently harmful to society. It is possible that a strategic, benevolent fake news campaign would actually encourage prosocial behavior. If, for example, we could somehow convince everyone that hatred made your hair fall out, more people might actively work to address their anti-Black, anti-immigrant, xenophobic, and white supremacist sentiments.

As a historical rule, the United States does not seem to have a problem with fakery. Accusations about what constitutes unacceptable fakeness typically fall along ideological lines. In the present political context, this line is often that which is perceived to be between Democrats and Republicans. Author and philosopher Frantz Fanon (1965) suggested another dialectic, the line between the colonized and the colonizer. He argued,

> The problem of truth ought also to be considered. In every age, among the people, truth is the property of the national cause. . . . The native replies to the living lie of the colonial situation by an equal falsehood. . . . Truth is that which hurries on the breakup of the colonialist regime; it is that which promotes the emergence of the nation. . . . In this colonialist context there is no truthful behavior: and the good is quite simply that which is evil for "them." (p. 39)

In this chapter, we speak as and with the colonized. From this perspective, we hope that this chapter supports the critical thinking skills, racial literacies, and sociopolitical consciousness necessary to produce, identify, and interpret information that "hurries on the breakup of the colonialist regime." That information is real news.

In contrast, fake news includes intentional efforts to characterize social relationships in ways that demean or discredit people of color in our struggles for recognition. It encompasses all of the delays, omissions, outright lies, misrepresentations, and manipulations that alter how oppressed people might understand and advocate to improve their political situation. Fake news presents the world in ways that makes oppression seem normal and inevitable.

In what follows, we offer three historical moments that exemplify how fake news has been used to control and coerce African and African-descended people in the United States. Similar arguments could (and should) be made for First Nation and Indigenous peoples, native Hawaiians, Latinx communities, Asian and Asian American peoples, immigrants of color, women of color, and any of the above who are also poor, queer, differently abled, or non-Christian.

The first historical moment identifies the delays and omissions that prevented news of the Emancipation Proclamation from reaching enslaved Black people in Texas and elsewhere. The second historical moment addresses the outright lies and misrepresentations that ostracized left-leaning Black activists during the Red Scare. The final historical moment summarizes Russian interference in online Black Lives Matter communities through manipulation on social media.

THE EMANCIPATION PROCLAMATION

President Abraham Lincoln issued the Emancipation Proclamation on January 1, 1863, a hundred days after a preliminary announcement that detailed the scope of the executive order (Jeffries, 2004). The document extended legal freedom to enslaved Black people in secessionist territories that were not already under Union control. Tens of thousands of Black people under Confederate jurisdiction experienced an immediate shift in their legal status. This shift did not occur, however, in eastern regions of Texas, where Black people continued to labor in the chattel slavery system for two additional years (Wiggins, 1990).

It was not until June 19, 1865, that Union Army Major General Gordon Granger and approximately 2,000 Union soldiers arrived in Galveston, TX, to announce that the tide of the Civil War had turned and that life beyond plantations was a possibility. General Order No. 3 read in part:

> The people of Texas are informed that, in accordance with a proclamation from the Executive of the United States, "all slaves are free." This involves an

> absolute equality of personal rights and rights of property between former masters and slaves, and the connection heretofore existing between them becomes that between employer and hired labor. (Texas State Library and Archives Commission, 2017, para. 2).

The order also instructed that the formerly enslaved were to "remain quietly at their present homes," to "work for wages," and to avoid "idleness" (Texas State Library and Archives Commission, 2017, para. 2).

As could be expected, various spontaneous celebrations occurred as Black people began to make sense of the revised racial order (Hume & Arceneaux, 2008; Jeffries, 2004; Wiggins, 1990). The hope that many in the Black community experienced on June 19, 1865, cannot be understated. These celebrations would eventually be commemorated as "Juneteenth."

As late as the 1960s, author and activist Ralph Ellison used Juneteenth as a metaphor for "the United States' capacity for regeneration" in a posthumously published novel about race, identity, and memory (Hobson, 2005, p. 626). Juneteenth became a recognized state holiday in Texas in 1978 and is acknowledged to varying degrees in cities across the United States (Wiggins, 1990).

As with most holidays, origin stories about Juneteenth are tapestries of archival records and ancestral imagination. Mythologies include accounts of a nameless Black Union soldier traveling to the southwest from Washington, DC, by mule. Another folktale describes the lynching of a messenger tasked with delivering the news of emancipation (Wiggins, 1990).

These remembered accounts draw on the violent suppression and distortion of information (and literacy resources) in Black communities. They force us to remember that throughout enslavement, truth and the tools to ascertain truth were systemically violently subverted for Black people. This subversion was not always through the promotion of verifiable falsehoods, but through inaction, withholding, and the dissemination of partial information.

In addition to the likely threat of violence, there were multiple other possible barriers to the timely dissemination of the Emancipation Proclamation in Texas. Even as the Civil War raged to the north and east, many Texan soldiers were preoccupied with the violent colonial conquest and administration of Indigenous people and land to the south. Texas newspapers struggled with declining resources, staff, and wartime obstacles to distribution (Cronin, 2008).

All of these factors would bear relevance if Black *and* White people were similarly unaware of Lincoln's decree. This, however, was not the case. News of the Emancipation Proclamation was intentionally delayed in Black communities in Texas through suppression and deceit.

In 1863 a Texas slave owner reported beating and shooting his "black wretches" for refusing to work. He was so overwhelmed by the insubordinations he contemplated selling the slaves and working "with [his] hands!" (Addington, 1950, p. 430). As late as January 1865 a Texas cavalry colonel made his intentions regarding the Proclamation clear. He stated he would "never give [my slaves] up until I am obliged to, and that will be a long time." He then assured fellow White Southerners, "you and your children [would] be waited upon by slaves as long as you all live" (Levine, 2006, p. 82).

Murder and the celebrated perpetuity of Black enslavement are disorienting and common on lists of the atrocities of slavery. Unique in this case is the fact that as of the slave owner and colonel's respective declarations, there were no legal slaves in Texas.

The slave owner and the colonel reasoned about their condition as White men, as well as the condition of Black Texans, based on fake news. Omitted from their reasoning was the legal, political, and military information that had altered racial power dynamics in Texas. While they chose to ignore this information, they actively withheld it from the Black people they shot and subordinated. Even after the Battle of Appomattox Courthouse, which ended the Civil War, slave owners in Texas (and elsewhere) lied about a Confederate victory and continuance of the institution of slavery (Levine, 2013).

Sometime between 1936 and 1938, Tempie Cummins was interviewed for the Federal Writers' Project. Cummins, who had been enslaved on a plantation in Jasper, Texas, recalled the day her mother discovered that they were legally free:

> Mother was workin' in the house, and she cooked too. She say she used to hide in the chimney corner and listen to what the white folks say. When freedom was 'clared, marster wouldn' tell 'em, but mother she hear him tellin' mistus that the slaves was free but they didn' know it and he's not gwineter tell 'em till he makes another crop or two. When mother hear that she say she slip out the chimney corner and crack her heels together four times and shouts, 'I's free, I's free.' Then she runs to the field, 'gainst marster's will and tol' all the other slaves and they quit work. Then she run away and in the night she slip into a big ravine near the house and have them bring me to her. Marster, he come out with his gun and shot at mother but she run down the ravine and gits away with me. (quoted in Berlin, Favreau, & Miller, 2011)

The human cost of fake news in the story of Juneteenth is inconceivable. The political cost is no less great: a 2-year delay in free Black people's efforts to advocate for transitional services, reparations, and equal recognition under the law. Political scientist Judson Jeffries (2004) has suggested that these early fake news stories were only intended to sustain slavery for one or two more harvest seasons. Yet many of these stories have very real echoes even today.

THE COLD WAR

Civil rights gains during the Cold War are often attributed to the U.S. government's efforts to polish its democratic image as it fought a series of ideological battles with the Communist Soviet Union. Yet the policy of containing Communism did not always lead to greater rights for the Black community in the United States, especially when containment was used to discredit and control ideas, movements, or persons considered subversive to the political, economic, and racial status quo.

By 1949, African American singer, actor, and activist Paul Robeson had long been under investigation by anti-Communist government officials who viewed his dedication to civil rights and outspoken criticism of colonialism in Africa as subversive. His speech questioning cold war politics at the 1949 Partisans of Peace Conference at the Salle Pleyel in Paris marks the moment Western media began to regularly portray him as a "Communist sympathizer" (Cygan, 1999, p. 31). Robeson said,

> We in America do not forget that it was on the backs of the white workers from Europe and on the backs of millions of blacks that the wealth of America was built. And we are resolved to share it equally. We reject any hysterical raving that urges us to make war on anyone. (quoted in Callow, 2018, para. 12)

Within days of the conference, the Associated Press misquoted Robeson, changing his speech to something quite different:

> We denounce the policy of the United States government, which is similar to that of Hitler and Goebbels. . . . It is unthinkable that American Negroes would go to war on behalf of those who have oppressed us for generations against a country [the Soviet Union] which in one generation has raised our people to the full dignity of mankind. (quoted in Iton, 2008, p. 36)

Almost immediately, newspaper headlines accused him of being a "Communist traitor" (King, 2011). A *New York Times* article bore the headline, "'BLACK STALIN' AIM IS LAID TO ROBESON; Ex-Red Official Says Singer, a Communist, Suffered 'Delusions of Grandeur.'" The article began, "[Robeson], Negro singer and actor, was identified as a member of the Communist party 'for many years' today by a former member of the national committee of that party" (The New York Times, 1949).

Black government informants described Robeson as "the voice of the Kremlin" and "Black Stalin" (Mack, 2006, p. 162). Eventually, Black activists including Mary McLeod Bethune, A. Philip Randolph, Jackie Robinson, and Adam Clayton Powell, Jr., engaged in public denouncements of Robeson.

Robeson denied membership in the Communist Party in 1946 before officials in California, and continued to do so in his memoir: "The truth is: *I am not and never have been involved in any international conspiracy or any other kind, and do not know anyone who is*" (1958, p. 38; italics in original). In his testimony before the House of Representatives Un-American Activities Committee, he explained that his speech reflected his belief that "it was healthy for Americans to consider whether or not Negroes should fight for people who kick them around" (Hearings Before the Committee on Un American Activities, 1966, p. 42).

It was too late. The material consequences that followed the spread of these false claims were "devastating" for Robeson's life and career (Mack, 2006, p. 162). Federal scrutiny and harassment increased, the media branded him disloyal and unpatriotic, and the State Department revoked his passport from 1950 to 1958.

This pattern of using cold war politics to falsely label and discredit resistance to racial injustice continued through the 1960s. In particular,

> as Southern McCarthyites equated black self-assertion with a Marxist plot to destroy America, the WCC [White Citizens' Council] and the KKK claimed desegregation efforts would lead to "mongrelization" and "amalgamation." The powerful cocktail of anti-Communism, white supremacy, and sexualized propaganda and paranoia enabled whites to push aside or even kill African Americans who asserted their humanity. (McGuire, 2010, p. 77)

However, the assertion of humanity by African Americans, and the ever-present backlash, was not confined to southern states.

Following the "Long Hot Summer" of 1967, the HUAC sought to create a false narrative around the urban unrest events (i.e., race "riots") that took place in 164 cities, including Detroit, Newark, Tampa, and Minneapolis. Titled "Subversive Influences in Riots, Looting, and Burning," the committee presented, as Exhibit No. 2, excerpts from J. Edgar Hoover's testimony before the House Appropriations Subcommittee earlier that year. His testimony falsely attributed "racial unrest" to the "success of this Communist smear campaign in popularizing the cry of 'police brutality' to the point where it has been accepted by many individuals having no affiliation with or sympathy for the Communist movement" (HUAC, 1966, p. 883).

As a public hearing, this exhibit disseminated misinformation directly in contrast to the findings of the Kerner Commission one year later:

> On the basis of all the information collected, the Commission concludes that: The urban disorders of the summer of 1967 were not caused by, nor were they the consequence of, any organized plan or "conspiracy." Specifically, the Commission has found no evidence that all or any of the disorders or the incidents that led to them were planned or directed by any organization or group, international, national, or local. (Wilentz, 2016, p. 9)

Instead, the Kerner Commission concluded that "Our Nation is moving toward two societies, one black, one white—separate and unequal" (Wilentz, 2016, p. 1). Against the widespread belief that Communist infiltration had led to the "riots," the commission further elaborated, "White society is deeply implicated in the ghetto. White institutions created it, white institutions maintain it, and white society condones it" (Wilentz, 2016, p. 2).

A bestseller when it was first published in 1968, the Kerner Report challenged the misinformation of the HUAC hearings; however, without inclusion into the official narratives of the United States, the still-relevant findings of the commission cannot provide a bulwark against the spread of fake news that continue to obscure the causes of racial unrest.

BLACK LIVES MATTER

After the 2013 acquittal of George Zimmerman for killing Trayvon Martin and the events surrounding Michael Brown and the 2014 Ferguson liberation movement, activists proclaiming "Black lives matter" reinvigorated debates about race, protest, and Black direct action in the United States. Black Lives Matter, now the Black Lives Matter Global Network (BLMGN), promotes change in societal structures that promote anti-Blackness (Cullors-Khan & Bandele, 2018; Garza, 2014; Taylor, 2016).

Similar to previous Black social movements, BLMGN supports the eradication of institutional racism, and police violence, and improvements in the criminal justice system. Black Lives Matter also seeks better treatment and the recognition of the humanity of Black women, Black queer people, Black immigrants, and other groups who historically have been excluded within Black social movements and public discourse. Black Lives Matter is a call to action in "talking about the ways in which Black people are deprived of their basic human rights and dignity" (Garza, 2014, para. 11).

Yet, for many people, the acknowledgement that Black lives matter is divisive and polarizing. Critics have complained that Black Lives Matter is exclusionary to other races, ethnicities, and cultures, even suggesting that the organization change its name to "All Lives Matter" or "Innocent Lives Matter" (McCarthy, 2015). Others believe that BLMGN is unnecessary and that problems with Black people or their communities are endemic or simply cases of bad individual choices. They believe that ideas that suggest U.S. structures and institutions are more or less violent or discriminatory based on race is a false narrative.

Therefore, many news stories, which tend to come from conservative outlets, about BLMGN have attempted to discredit the movement and blame it as the root cause of racial tension and police backlash. These news outlets also chastise BLMGN for not devoting its energy and resources to what they perceive are real Black issues like the constructed notion of "Black-on-Black crime" (Braga & Brunson, 2015; Wilson, 2005).

While "Black-on-Black crime" is used to purport the criminality of Black people in their own neighborhoods against their "own" people, it is the nexus between Black Lives Matter and crimes against White people that pique concerns for BLMGN opponents. For example, Scott Lattin, a White man from a small town in Texas, reported to his local police station that someone representing BLMGN vandalized his truck. He believed that his vehicle was targeted because he supported the police.

On his truck, he advertised "Police Lives Matter" and hung blue ribbons representing his support. The words, "Black Lives Matter" and the phrase, "Fuck your flag, your family, your feelings, your faith" were spray-painted on his vehicle (Chan, 2015, para. 6). The news story garnered national attention, and a GoFundMe page worth $6,000 was started to help Lattin purchase another truck. It was later revealed that Lattin had lied about Black Lives Matter as the instigators of the crime; he confessed that he vandalized his vehicle for insurance monies.

A second fake news story about Black Lives Matter were the events surrounding the Twitter hashtag #BLMkidnapping. In 2017 a White teenager, who was said to be disabled, was abducted and abused in Chicago by four Black teenagers. The kidnappers appear to have taken him to an apartment and terrorized him with a knife. The Black teenage kidnappers went live on Facebook's social media platform to archive the event.

The video captured the Black teenagers screaming, "Fuck White people" and "Fuck Donald Trump." Within 24 hours of the video, many people on Twitter connected the abductors to BLMGN, naming the incident with the hashtag #BLMkidnapping. The hashtag was mentioned over 400,000 times. However, no link between the kidnappers and BLMGN was ever found (Yan, Jones, & Almasy, 2017)

Additionally, BLMGN has been labeled a hate group that is antipolice. Conservative personalities have said that BLMGN is a terrorist group committing hate crimes, have claimed that it advocates killing Americans, and have compared it to the Klu Klux Klan (Bellware, 2015; Blake, 2016; Holmes, 2015; Mazza, 2016). Fox News even ran a graphic that described BLMGN as a "murder movement" and as a "radical group that calls for the killing of cops!" (Hanson & McCormack, 2015). Because of these commentaries, there have been reports of police retaliation, surveillance of BLM leaders by the Federal Bureau of Investigation (FBI), and a new FBI designation for those believed to be involved with BLMGN: Black Identity Extremists (BIE) (FBI, 2017; Patterson, 2017).

The FBI defined *Black Identity Extremists* as individuals "who seek, wholly or in part, through unlawful acts of violence . . . of establishing a separate black homeland or autonomous black social institutions, communities, or governing organizations within the United States" (FBI, 2017,

p. 2). The words *Black Lives Matter* were not directly mentioned, but the timeline of the investigation coincided with the same year as Michael Brown's death and the Ferguson liberation movement (Vozick-Levinson, 2014). The FBI assessed that it is very likely that BIE "spurred an increase in premeditated, retaliatory lethal violence against law enforcement" (FBI, 2017, p. 4).

Collectively, fake news concerning BLMGN as criminals and terrorists were effective tools for Russian interference during the 2016 U.S. presidential election (Byers, 2017). According to reports, Russian operatives bought Facebook advertisements representing BLMGN. Geographically focused on Ferguson, MO, and Baltimore, MD, based on the police killings of Michael Brown and Freddie Grey, these advertisements represented support for the organization but entailed divisive rhetoric to sow discontent with opponents.

While the advertisements have not been released to the general public, based on the histories we have presented, as well as the history of Soviet/Russian interference (Hughes, 1963) of Black civil rights in the United States, we can imagine the anti-Black sentiments articulated about BLMGN.

CONCLUSION

We believe that each of the above moments is evidence of a systemic fake news campaign that is intended to sustain a particular set of racial relationships. The interests of Black people were disregarded, manipulated, or caricatured to the point that they could be deemed illegitimate. There will always be white supremacists, Confederate apologists, and McCarthyists. Apparently, we can now add international cyber espionage artists to the list.

These folks will always attempt to represent the world in ways that makes the status quo seem permissible. Regardless of the breaking headline, the controversial tweet, or shocking footage, some will always insist that the status quo is not acceptable. If history has taught us anything, it is that each side will use its full force to prove that the other is faking it.

We hope that this chapter sparks conversation about the truths of the colonial situation and collective movement toward dismantling this situation. To conclude, we return to Fanon's (1965) argument: "In this colonialist context there is no truthful behavior: and the good is quite simply that which is evil for 'them'" (p. 50). Whether a news story is "real" or "fake" depends on the extent to which you identify as "us" or "them." We can call ourselves one nation, but let us keep it real: *Us* is the moral community with which you identify, and *them* is just about everyone else.

REFERENCES

Addington, W. G. (1950). Slave insurrections in Texas. *The Journal of Negro History, 35*, 408–434.

Allcott, H., & Gentzkow, M. (2017). Social media and fake news in the 2016 election. *Journal of Economic Perspectives, 31*, 211–36.

Bellware, K. (2015, October 22). Sean Hannity draws comparison between Black Lives Matter and KKK. *HuffPost*. Retrieved from www.huffingtonpost.com/entry/sean-hannity-black-lives-matter-kkk_us_5628ff2ee4b0ec0a38936571

Berlin, I., Favreau, M., & Miller, S. (Eds.). (2011). *Remembering slavery: African Americans talk about their personal experiences of slavery and emancipation* [Audio file]. Washington, DC: Library of Congress.

Blake, A. (2016, July 9). Limbaugh labels Black Lives Matter a "terrorist group" after Dallas shootings. *The Washington Times*. Retrieved from www.washingtontimes.com/news/2016/jul/9/limbaugh-labels-black-lives-matter-terrorist-group/

Braga, A. A., & Brunson, R. K. (2015). *The police and public discourse on "black on black" violence: Perspectives in policing bulletin*. Washington, DC: Department of Justice, National Institute of Justice.

Byers, D. (2017, September 28). Exclusive: Russian-bought Black Lives Matter ad on Facebook targeted Baltimore and Ferguson. *CNN Business*. Retrieved from money.cnn.com/2017/09/27/media/facebook-black-lives-matter-targeting/index.html

Callow, S. (2018, February 8). The emperor Robeson. *The New York Review of Books*. Retrieved from www.nybooks.com/articles/2018/02/08/emperor-paul-robeson/

Chan, M. (2015, September 19). Texas man vandalizes own truck with anti-police messages, blames it on Black Lives Matter activists: Cops. *[New York] Daily News*. Retrieved from www.nydailynews.com/news/national/man-vandalizes-truck-blames-black-lives-matter-article-1.2366871

Cronin, M. M. (2008). "War is thundering at our very gates": Texas newspapers during the Civil War. *Journalism History, 34*, 23–33.

Cullors-Khan, P., & Bandele, A. (2018). *When they call you a terrorist: A Black Lives Matter memoir*. New York, NY: St. Martin's Press.

Cygan, M. E. (1999). A man of his times: Paul Robeson and the press, 1924–1976. *Pennsylvania History: A Journal of Mid-Atlantic Studies, 66*, 27–46.

Fanon, F. (1965). *The wretched of the earth* (R. Philcox, Trans.). New York, NY: Grove Press.

Federal Bureau of Investigation. (2017). *Black identity extremists likely motivated to target law enforcement officers*. Washington, DC: Author.

Garza, A. (2014, October 7). A herstory of the #BlackLivesMatter movement. *The Feminist Wire*. Retrieved from thefeministwire.com/2014/10/blacklivesmatter-2/

Hanson, H., & McCormack, S. (2015, September 1). Fox News suggests Black Lives Matter is a "murder" movement, "hate group." *HuffPost*. Retrieved from www.huffingtonpost.com/entry/black-lives-matter-fox-news-hate-group_us_55e5c102e4b0b7a9633a3b12

Hearings Before the Committee on Un American Activities, House of Representatives, 90th Cong. 1 (1966).

Hobson, C. Z. (2005). Ralph Ellison, Juneteenth, and African American prophecy. *MFS Modern Fiction Studies*, *51*, 617–647.

Holmes, J. (2015, September 1). Last night Bill O'Reilly compared #BlacklivesMatter to the Ku Klux Klan. *Esquire*. Retrieved from www.esquire.com/news-politics/news/a37547/heres-a-clip-of-bill-oreilly-comparing-blacklivesmatter-to-the-ku-klux-klan/

Hughes, T. L. (1963, June 14). *Soviet media coverage of current US racial crisis* [Research Memorandum]. Washington, DC: Department of State..

Hume, J., & Arceneaux, N. (2008). Public memory, cultural legacy, and press coverage of the Juneteenth revival. *Journalism History*, *34*, 155–163.

Iton, R. (2008). *In search of the Black fantastic: Politics & popular culture in the post-civil rights era*. Oxford, United Kingdom: Oxford University Press.

Jeffries, J. L. (2004). Juneteenth, Black Texans, and the case for reparations. *Negro Educational Review*, *55*, 109–118.

King, G. (2011, Sept. 13). What Paul Robeson said. *Smithsonian.com*. Retrieved from www.smithsonianmag.com/history/what-paul-robeson-said-77742433/

Levine, B. (2006). *Confederate emancipation: Southern plans to free and arm slaves during the Civil War.* Oxford, United Kingdom: Oxford University Press.

Levine, B. (2013). *The fall of the House of Dixie: The Civil War and the social revolution that transformed the South*. New York, NY: Random House.

Mack, D. (2006). Hazel Scott: A career curtailed. *The Journal of African American History*, *91*, 153–170.

Mazza, E. (2016, May 26). Bill O'Reilly: Black Lives Matter is "killing Americans." *HuffPost*. Retrieved from www.huffingtonpost.com/entry/bill-oreilly-black-lives-matter_us_57465f7ee4b055bb1171385f

McCarthy, T. (2015, August 27). Rand Paul tells Black Lives Matter: Change your name and your tactics. *The Guardian*. Retrieved from www.theguardian.com/us-news/2015/aug/27/rand-paul-black-lives-matter-name-change-all-innocent

McGuire, D. L. (2010). *At the dark end of the street: Black women, rape, and resistance—a new history of the civil rights movement from Rosa Parks to the rise of Black power.* New York, NY: Vintage Books.

The New York Times. (1949, July 15). "Black Stalin" aim is laid to Robeson; ex-red official says singer, a communist, suffered "delusions of grandeur." *The New York Times*, p. 13. Available at www.nytimes.com/1949/07/15/archives/black-stalin-aim-is-laid-to-robeson-exred-official-says-singer-a.html

Patterson, B. E. (2017, October 19). Police spied on New York Black Lives Matter group, internal police documents show. *Mother Jones*. Retrieved from www.motherjones.com/crime-justice/2017/10/police-spied-on-new-york-black-lives-matter-group-internal-police-documents-show/

Robeson, P. (1958). *Here I stand.* Boston, MA: Beacon Press.

Taylor, K. Y. (2016). *From #BlackLivesMatter to Black liberation*. Chicago, IL: Haymarket Books.

Texas State Library and Archives Commission. (2017). Texas remembers: Juneteenth. Retrieved from www.tsl.texas.gov/ref/abouttx/juneteenth.html

Vozick-Levinson, S. (2014, December 16). Watch Ferguson freedom fighters share stories from frontlines. *Rolling Stone*. Retrieved from www.rollingstone.com/politics/videos/ferguson-freedom-fighters-a-day-in-the-life-20141216

Wiggins, W. H., Jr. (1990). *O freedom!: Afro-American emancipation celebrations.* Nashville, TN: University of Tennessee Press.

Wilentz, S. (Ed.). (2016). *The Kerner report: The national advisory commission on civil disorders.* Princeton, NJ: Princeton University Press.

Wilson, D. (2005). *Inventing black-on-black violence: Discourse, space, and representation.* Syracuse, NY: Syracuse University Press.

Yan, H., Jones, S., & Almasy, S. (2017, January 5). Chicago torture video: 4 charged with hate crimes, kidnapping. *CNN.* Retrieved from www.cnn.com/2017/01/05/us/chicago-facebook-live-beating/index.html

CHAPTER 3

Teens, Social Media, and Fake News

Ellen Middaugh

Since 2016 the term *fake news* has taken on many meanings. While the term was originally employed in response to wholly fabricated news stories introduced into the social media ecosystem, its usage has spread to information that one believes to be biased, limited in perspective, exaggerated, or a blend of fact and fiction. Furthermore, the term has been routinely employed by members of the current presidential administration to refer to news that they believe to unfairly cast the administration in a negative light. These many uses of the term fake news illustrate the challenge of civic media literacy education.

Assessments of *credibility*—whether a source legitimately represents the issue being written about—involve more than simple factual accuracy. Rather, definitions of credibility have included fairly objective criteria such as comprehensiveness, recency, accuracy, and author credentials, as well as judgments about the motives of the author and whether those motives align with the best interests of the reader. Additionally, research on credibility has noted that personal experience has an impact on perception of and emotional response to information (Metzger & Flanagin, 2015).

Research on social media has also found that social cues may play a strong role in assessments of credibility of news accessed through social media. Youth have cited the reactions of friends, families, public figures, and strangers, as well as *virality*—whether the news is shared by multiple sources—as cues regarding the credibility of information (Clark & Marchi, 2017). A large-scale survey of adults found that those with higher comfort with social media in general were also more likely to cite relying on the opinions of others in their assessments of credibility of news (Flanagin, Hocevar, & Samahito, 2014).

Given the complexity of judging the trustworthiness of news, it is not surprising that a recent survey of teens found that less than half (44%) reported feeling confident they could tell fake news from real news (Robb, 2017). While there is little reason to believe that youth bear the brunt of the responsibility for the current climate of misinformation, there is plenty of evidence that youth need support in this area. Furthermore, adolescent and emerging adult development may encourage susceptibility to misinformation, but it is also an opportunity to develop skills, dispositions, and habits that are better adapted to the current climate than what is typical for adults.

The purpose of this chapter is to provide context for educators from research that focuses on the youth perspective. Specifically, I seek to do the following:

- Provide an overview of teen media habits, with a focus on recent statistics related to news consumption
- Draw on developmental research to describe how changes in social, emotional, and cognitive development that occur in adolescence and early adulthood may intersect with the task of learning to better assess the credibility of information
- Make recommendations for developmentally appropriate media literacy education for youth

Readers are encouraged to consider how youth can be invited into the process of creating better solutions to the challenge of fake news. The primary goal of identifying the interaction of adolescent and emerging adult developmental changes with news habits is not to work against youth tendencies but to meet youth where they are and create more engaging and effective educational interventions.

YOUTH SOCIAL MEDIA HABITS

As media platforms have evolved, so have youth media habits. At this current moment, the best way to describe youth social media use is that for most teens, social media use involves multiple platforms with differentiated use. Since 2009, nationally representative surveys have found that a large majority of U.S. youth are active users of social media (Madden et al., 2013; NORC, 2017). What has primarily changed over the last decade is a growing trend toward differentiated use of multiple platforms and a change in the most prominent platforms.

For example, a 2015 survey found that 76% of teens (and 81% of older teens) used social media, and 71% used two or more sites (Lenhart, 2015). While Facebook was easily the most popular platform in 2015, used by 71% of teens (compared to the next platform at 52%), what has changed in the last 2 to 3 years is the emergence of Instagram and Snapchat as the most popular platforms, used by at least 75% of teens each, and the use of multiple platforms (Instagram, Snapchat, and Facebook) by a majority of teens (NORC, 2017).

These findings should not be surprising to anyone who spends time with teenagers. However, relevant to the problem of misinformation, it is worth noting a discrepancy between the platforms that are receiving the greatest level of scrutiny for their contributions to misinformation, Facebook and Twitter, and the platforms most commonly used by teens, Instagram and Snapchat. Recently, under significant public scrutiny, Facebook has begun experimenting with algorithm options to limit the spread of false news (Pierson & Lien, 2018), and Twitter has begun to remove suspected fake accounts (Scola, 2018). To date, however, Instagram and Snapchat have not instituted such measures.

Studies have emerged to examine how youth access news, through which platforms, and their habits related to vetting the credibility of news that they receive through social media. Recent studies have suggested that social media serves as a mechanism for incidental news exposure. A 2015 national survey of millennials (aged 18–34) found that Facebook was either the primary or secondary gateway through which participants reported becoming aware of news (American Press Institute, 2015). Among younger millennials, there was a stronger tendency to get news from social media, distributed across multiple platforms such as Twitter, Reddit, and Instagram.

A 2017 national survey of teens and tweens (aged 10–17) found that among social media users, 76% reported getting news through Facebook and YouTube (Robb, 2017), reinforcing the conclusion that Facebook plays a major role in exposing youth to news but that other social media platforms do as well. These trends do not suggest that youth rely solely on social media for news; both studies found that youth were aware of the need to follow up and go to other sources, particularly for "hard news" about serious social or political topics. However, social media does appear to play a substantial role in introducing youth to the news.

In light of the importance of social media to youth news consumption, it is comforting to know that the majority are aware of the need to pay attention to sources. Young adults in the aforementioned survey of millennials reported that they typically followed up on news stories received through social media by searching for additional information or going directly to news sites to check, filtering for sites they knew or sites with transparent links to sources (American Press Institute, 2015). Among teens who reported getting news through social media, more than two-thirds reported that they paid attention to the source of the news (Robb, 2017).

Though it is heartening to see that youth are aware of the importance of paying attention to the legitimacy of news, it is also clear that the practice of vetting news is challenging. Compared to 83% of adult survey participants who recently reported feeling confident in their ability to tell if news is fake (Barthell, Mitchell, & Holcomb, 2016), only 44% of teens agreed that they could tell the difference between real and fake news (Robb, 2017). Studies of youth reasoning about the credibility of online websites have found that many struggle to balance multiple and conflicting indicators (e.g., McGrew, Breakstone, Ortega, Smith, & Wineburg, 2018; McGrew, Ortega, Breakstone, & Wineburg, 2017).

Finally, it is important to remember that youth do not simply consume news media, but that many also comment, produce, and share news. How youth make decisions about what to share and the role of credibility of news in their comments and creations is an important component of their developing relationship to news. In addressing the problem of fake news, educating youth to be more effective consumers is only part of the solution. There is also a need for education about responsible production, commentary, and sharing of media.

How people make decisions about what news to share has been studied in far less depth than evaluation of credibility of news that is consumed. Recent surveys have found that 31% of youth who shared news in the last 6 months (Robb, 2017) and 23% of all adults have shared false or made-up stories (Barthell et al., 2016). Interestingly, 14% of the adult participants reported knowingly sharing false stories, which suggests that teens and young adults are somewhat aware of their role in feeding into the circulation of misinformation, but that finding does not provide much insight into how they make those decisions in action.

To summarize, the research suggests that the near ubiquitous use of social media among teens across multiple platforms has led to social media playing an important role in determining what news youth receive, that youth understand the importance of verifying news but struggle with doing so effectively, and that youth also contribute to misinformation by sharing false media stories. The finding that youth often first encounter news through social media and then go to other sources reinforces the argument of media studies scholars Lynn Clark and Regina Marchi (2017) that it is more common in the era of social media for youth to allow news to bubble up and come to them.

ADOLESCENT DEVELOPMENT AND YOUTH INTERACTION WITH ONLINE NEWS

While there has been increasing attention to youth news practices and efforts to develop assessments and interventions to support use of online information in reasoning about civic issues (e.g., Hobbs, 2011; Martens & Hobbs, 2015; McGrew, Breakstone et al., 2018; McGrew, Ortega, et al., 2017), the majority of these efforts have not explicitly taken into account aspects of adolescent development that lead youth to be more interested in consuming and sharing news that fits under the umbrella of fake news (i.e., news that uses exaggerated language, appeals to emotion, lacks balanced perspectives, or relies on anecdotal or unverifiable evidence).

Over 50 years of research in adolescent development has found that a combination of adolescent and emerging adults' continuing brain development and their changing status in society lead to a variety of differences in how youth process social information, coordinate reasoning and action, assert their autonomy, and engage in identity exploration compared to older adults (Steinberg, 2017). Some scholars have begun to articulate how these trends influence youth online behavior (Davis, 2013; Konijn, Veldhuis, Plasier, Spekman, & den Hamer, 2015).

These insights from developmental research provide a useful lens for explaining and interpreting observed patterns in how youth reason about and interact with media, such as struggling to apply multiple credibility cues at once (McGrew, Ortega, et al., 2017) or being drawn to personal anecdotes or sensational headlines (Clark & Marchi, 2017).

The Role of Experience and Expertise in Reasoning

If youth know the importance of assessing the credibility of news and information and have been taught strategies for doing so, why are they so vulnerable to making mistakes in judging accurate versus inaccurate news? For example, recent research of youth online civic reasoning found that when asked to perform a variety of tasks assessing the credibility of online sources, only 8–18% of middle and high school students and 30–31% of college students demonstrated mastery of those tasks (McGrew, Breakstone, et al., 2018).

One possible conclusion from such a finding is that youth need to be taught additional strategies for assessing the credibility of information, but the authors note that just focusing on students is not sufficient, as adolescents struggle with knowing what, among many cues, is relevant to attend to across a range of situations (McGrew, Ortega, et al., 2017). What is interesting is that research on adolescent cognitive development suggests that youth should have many of the reasoning capabilities needed to complete such a task, but they do not apply them in practice.

Adolescence is noted for being a period of rapidly expanding cognitive capabilities and a time in which changes to the structure and function of the brain occur (Steinberg, 2017). Of particular relevance for assessing news is the ability to think in multiple dimensions, which research has found improves considerably during adolescence (Kuhn, 2009). The ability to weigh multiple criteria when assessing news requires attention not just to facts, but also to potential alternative interpretations, author motivation, and the implications of the facts for making judgments about social issues.

Developmental research suggests that adolescence is not only a time when individuals can learn to manage the complexity of reasoning about online information, but that it is also an important time to practice doing so because of the heightened malleability of the brain (Selemon, 2013). These skills can be more challenging to learn later in adulthood. However, just because adolescents and young adults *can* engage in multidimensional thinking, research suggests that very few adolescents (or adults, for that matter) typically reason with maximum capability in daily life.

Research has found large gaps between reasoning ability (how one performs when given a task) and reasoning in everyday situations (Kahneman, 2011). In the context of assessing the credibility of information, communications scholars Miriam Metzger and Andrew Flanagin (2015) have argued that it is more common for people to rely on heuristics and gut feelings than to engage in effortful analysis, which may be explained by both motivation and background knowledge. Research on adult use of strategies to assess the credibility of online information has found that people who have expertise on the topic are more likely to employ multiple credibility cues and rely less on factors such as the appearance or layout of the media (Flanagin & Metzger, 2007).

Additionally, research has found that adults are more likely to pay attention to the credibility of information when the issue is of personal salience and is perceived to be consequential (Byerly & Brodie, 2005). If expertise (background knowledge and experience) and salience lead to greater effort in assessing credibility, then the question is whether youth typically encounter news about which they have knowledge and feel that it matters whether the news is accurate.

Unfortunately, studies have found that many adolescents are frustrated because the news does not address the issues that matter most to them (Clark & Marchi, 2017; Robb, 2017). It is worth noting that in the Stanford History Education Group's (McGrew, Breakstone, et al., 2018) study of online reasoning the tasks exposed youth to typical news media but included many topics with which youth are unlikely to have had much experience or direct expertise, perhaps explaining, at least in part, their mistakes in judgment.

Outrage Language, Emotional Regulation, and Identity Work

Another concern raised about social media and news is the growing use of outrage discourse within news stories and in commentary as news is shared (Berry & Sobieraj, 2014). The term *outrage discourse* is used to capture language intended to provoke strong emotional responses (e.g., anger, disgust, moral indignation, and so on) through a range of tactics such as providing misleading facts, overgeneralizations, and personal attacks on the person in the story. Research has found a growing presence of this type of discourse in the media over time (Berry & Soberiaj, 2014).

Cable news and talk radio have been identified as the primary drivers of the increase in outrage discourse (Sobieraj & Berry, 2011), but as it becomes easier to share clips and quotations, often decontextualized from the source, social media may increase access to news sources that people may previously have ignored. Indeed, a 2011 survey of youth aged 15–25 found that those who access news through participatory media (social media or media shared through online social networks) were more likely to report having seen exchanges marked by outrage language (Middaugh, Bowyer, & Kahne, 2017).

Given the likelihood of exposure to outrage language and its role in creating a culture of misinformation, it is important to gain a better understanding of how youth interact with such news media. From a developmental perspective, there are several aspects of cognitive and social development that may influence their tendency to attend to or share news that employs outrage discourse, sensational headlines, or dramatic language.

Youth Brain Development and Reactions to Outrage Language

Thanks to advances in the ability to study changes in brain anatomy, researchers have learned that the brain undergoes significant reorganization during adolescence (Selemon, 2013), which partially helps explain what parents and teachers may see as an exasperating tendency to act before thinking or to be dramatic or emotional.

Adolescents *do* often act before thinking, which is explained in part by changes in the limbic system and prefrontal cortex that lead them to temporarily experience heightened sensitivity to rewards and emotions while still developing the cognitive control needed to resist the urge to act on first impulse (Dwyer et al., 2014). Applying these findings to media use and impact, scholars have hypothesized the resulting increase in sensation seeking may lead youth to seek out risky media or share media that gets attention or "likes" from peers, thus providing a social reward (Konijn, Veldhuis, et al., 2015).

Empirical research examining these effects have primarily focused on how teens respond to receiving positive feedback online, with participants in functional magnetic resonance imaging studies showing more activation of the reward centers of the brain not only when receiving positive feedback from peers (Guyer, McClure-Tone, Shiffrin, Pine, & Nelson, 2009) but also when viewing media that has many "likes" (compared to media with fewer "likes"), suggesting the social reward does not have to be direct (Sherman, Payton, Hernandez, Greenfield, & Dipretto, 2016). The latter study also found that cognitive control mechanisms were less likely to be activated while viewing risky media.

While research has not directly examined adolescent brain activity when processing news media, cognitive development has been applied to explain adolescents' interest in media that adults frequently identify as "offensive" or risqué (Steinberg, 2017; Valkenburg & Peter, 2013). While the emotional reward of watching crude television shows, violent movies, or

YouTube prank videos may be more related to the thrill of getting away with something parents do not entirely approve of or the social reward of peers' reactions, certain types of news media that fall into this category may also be rewarding and engaging due to feeding anger or fear.

For example, regardless of political perspective, language used by President Trump is often bold, designed to insult an opponent or can be read as having a double entendre. Whether this type of discourse sparks a thrill of seeing language that is discouraged by teachers and parents, anger at the message, or a sense of mischief in seeking out media against which some parents may feel strongly, the current political climate provides many opportunities for an emotional response from teens and adults alike.

What is not yet clear from the research is whether teens gravitate toward outrage media more than other media or more so than adults. Clark and Marchi's (2017) ethnographic research with youth found some preference for news media that uses strong, emotionally evocative language. They interpreted these findings as a preference for a sense of urgency and moral clarity when discussing important issues. However, given the sensitivity of the teen brain to strong emotions and a tendency to seek out such experiences, it is possible that the emotion evoked through outrage language may serve as a motivating force in media use.

Addressing the question of whether news media evokes an emotional response, Common Sense Media (Robb, 2017) found that 63% of tweens and teens surveyed reported feeling angry, depressed, or fearful in response to news they had read. In a forthcoming study drawing on data from the *2013 Youth Participatory Politics Survey* (Cohen & Kahne, 2018), I found that 58% of youth aged 15–25 reported feeling angry after reading a hypothetical Facebook exchange about the issue of income inequality that employed personal insults (Middaugh, 2018a). The question, then, is how these emotional responses influence processing of news and subsequent behavior.

Studies that have examined the impact of emotion on assessments of credibility come to somewhat mixed conclusions. Studies have found that adults report more cognitive engagement with negative stimuli (Valentino, Hutchings, Banks, & Davis, 2008; Valkenburg & Peter, 2013) but are only more likely to seek out additional information when made to feel anxious and actually seek out less additional information when made to feel angry (Valentino et al., 2008).

Additionally, media psychologists Elly Konijn, Juliette Walma van der Molen, and Sander van Nes (2009) found that all participants, but particularly teen participants, were more likely to assess documentary clips as factually accurate when experiencing negative emotions while watching. This research suggests that teens experience a high degree of reward stimulation in response to risky media, media that has been socially rewarded, or media that evokes emotion and that such experiences may interfere with judgments of credibility.

Consuming and Sharing News as Identity Exploration

Another potential influence on how youth interact with outrage news may be related to identity exploration, which is considered to be a key area of transformation in adolescence (Erikson, 1968). Due to both greater cognitive capacity and also changing social status, questions like Who am I? What is my place in the world? and Who is my community? are actively explored with new energy during adolescence and emerging adulthood. Media has long been identified as playing a critical role in this process by giving youth access to a range of possible identities, allowing them to test out and display an identity, and encouraging affiliation with certain groups of peers (Subrahmanyam & Šmahel, 2011).

Social media has been identified as an important tool for identity exploration as it provides opportunities to seek out a wider range of role models than may be available through traditional media and also because it allows for opportunities to explore and perform different identities in a wide range of contexts and to get feedback from others (Konijn, Veldhuis, et al., 2015; Spies Shapiro & Margolin, 2014). Racial, ethnic, religious, and sexual minority youth can find role models who may not be available through mainstream media and may access others who share their interests and allow them to identify with a group.

Applying these ideas to how youth interact with news through social media, Clark and Marchi (2017) observed their youth participants' desire to "write themselves into the news," by sharing news that aligns with their identity (as a person who cares about certain things or affiliates with certain communities) and commenting on news as they share it. This tendency aligns with psychologists Lauren Spies Shapiro and Gayla Margolin's (2014) observation that the access to an audience through social media supports teens in their developmental tasks to both stand out and fit in.

Clark and Marchi (2017) observed that by sharing media that takes a strong stance in a public or semipublic forum, youth were able to establish an aspect of their civic identity and get feedback from others in response. Additionally, by sharing media that was "liked" or commented on, they also demonstrated belonging with a group who shared their interests. While both acts are useful to civic identity development, they at times led to greater attention to the headlines with strong clear statements that would generate comments and "likes," leading young people to prefer sensational or emotionally evocative media.

Thus the elements of social media that are supportive of identity development can also promote greater attention to news that falls into the category of outrage media. The question for educators is not how to sidestep the natural tendencies of adolescents who want to assert identity and seek peer feedback, but how to take those tendencies into account when working to support news media practices.

Expanding Autonomy, Moral Critique, and Distrust of Authority

Another area of concern when discussing misinformation is the mistrust of institutional or authoritative news sources. Assessments of credibility do not just involve attention to facts and differences of perspective, but they also often involve some assessment of the intentions of the source and whether they have the readers' best interests at heart (Metzger & Flanagin, 2015). With the political polarization of media, this aspect of the judgment of credibility has led some to dismiss entire news organizations and the stories that come from them as fake or biased news. It is no longer the case that most U.S. citizens put their trust in institutionalized organizations that hold themselves and each other accountable to journalistic standards and practices.

History and youth development are colliding when it comes to the mistrust of authority in media. During adolescence, there are several transitions that may lead youth to be critical of institutional news and therefore likely to seek out user-generated news or anecdotal evidence. First, the cognitive changes discussed previously are believed to account for the growing tendency for adolescents to begin to question authority in a range of settings (Smetana & Villalobos, 2009). The ability to understand that others may have different motives and perspectives than their own and to have some understanding of what those perspectives may be can promote a tendency to question the legitimacy of parent and teacher authority, as well as social rules (Smetana & Villalobos, 2009). Applying this tendency to news media, this expanded capacity allows youth to recognize flaws in media coverage, such as biased coverage of one group over another, and to reflect on their own status and how they are portrayed in the media.

Additionally, the economic and legal status of many youth creates conditions in which they have relatively little input into or control over the institutions that organize their lives; therefore, they may have some justified critiques of how they are portrayed and treated (Ginwright & Cammarota, 2006). Indeed, the Common Sense Media survey (Robb, 2017) of tweens and teens found that not only were participants dissatisfied by the lack of coverage of issues that were most relevant to them, but 74% were also frustrated by their media representation.

This critique is echoed in Clark and Marchi's (2017) ethnographic research. They found that the kinds of news that were of most interest to their participants included topics that traditional news media sources, which they deem legacy media, may be actively discouraged from covering. For example, local events that got the attention of students, such as a controversial speaker or the changing of a bus route that students rely on, were scarcely covered by local news. Additionally, their participants noted frustration that the news shared information about problems but offered no practical advice or links to resources to further educate them about the issue.

This phenomenon is not due to news media failing to consider the perspectives of youth as much as it is a case where the news that youth expressed interest in held contradictory qualities to what most news outlets would prioritize (i.e., news of interest to a broad audience that takes an objective reporting stance). In this kind of case, information produced and shared by the local community through social media is the only news available.

In addition to critiques about whether traditional news sources serve their interests by covering news that is relevant, youth have also been critical of what they perceive as racial and gender bias in news media coverage (Robb, 2017). Not trusting the potential spin of traditional news media outlet coverage, in some cases, as noted by Clark and Marchi (2017), leads youth to prefer media that is directly from the source. Raw footage of events or firsthand accounts, which by definition are limited to a single perspective and anecdotal evidence, can also appear as a more unvarnished or pure news source.

Most adults are not blind to the challenges of news media coverage, but adolescents who are newly aware of these biases and limitations may weigh them more heavily. Adolescents' skepticism and perceptions of bias are a useful reminder to adults that limitations that many have taken for granted as inevitable should be noted and challenged. On the other hand, it can lead to a dismissal of traditional news outlets as irrelevant or hopelessly broken. The challenge to educators, then, is to figure out how to engage youth in both their moral critique and an appreciation of what the traditional standards of news media can offer. Additionally, turning a critical lens on social media in a manner that does not simply appeal to authority may also serve these purposes.

A Note of Caution Against Teen-Proofing Approaches

As described above, adolescents' and emerging adults' level of experience with and background knowledge related to news, their sensitivity to social and emotional rewards related to consuming and sharing certain types of media, and their critiques of the motives and priorities of news media outlets are all factors that may influence their judgments about fake news. These factors are not limited to this age period, but given the cognitive and social changes that are rapidly taking place, this period is considered a sensitive time in which there is greater flexibility, which leads to some vulnerability but also a significant opportunity for learning (Steinberg, 2014).

It may be tempting, in light of the description of how aspects of youth development create challenges in assessing the credibility of information and preferences for outrage media or anecdotal firsthand accounts, to simply limit students to a set of approved sources or to repeatedly stress certain strategies or values for assessing information while waiting for them to become adults. However, this approach not only misses a developmental window of opportunity, but it is also likely to be counterproductive as it will teach youth to conform to classroom expectations but not to engage in questioning and refining their own processes.

If youth only use approved sources or apply a set of strategies (e.g., using mainstream news media or government websites), they do not practice and reflect on the effectiveness of their own strategies for vetting news. Additionally, when youth only use "reputable sources," they may find that the issue they most care about is not covered by recent news or that research is represented with a limited perspective. Such tactics sidestep rather than directly engage what youth are thinking about and grappling with when they encounter news outside of school.

An alternative approach is to meet youth where they are and support their exploration in ways that lead them to come to their own conclusions. This process will be far easier if youth are given the opportunity to find, create, and share news related to issues with which they have expertise; to practice media literacy strategies across multiple contexts; and to acknowledge moral critique and limitations of "real" news as an entry point.

IMPLICATIONS FOR EDUCATION

Research on youth journalism and youth-led organizing has demonstrated that when investigating issues they care about, adolescents show a high degree of motivation for researching and analyzing information. For example, when investigating issues of high personal relevance and experience such as the adequacy of school bus service (Clark & Marchi, 2017), decisions to opt out of standardized testing (Soep, 2015), or school policies (Kirshner, 2015), ethnographic research has documented teens' critical thinking, concern for facts and evidence, and awareness of audience.

In a setting where youth explore issues with which they have direct experience and a personal stake, some of the challenges of credibility may be addressed. First, such an approach addresses the challenges of lack of background knowledge and salience that research has found leads to less attention to quality of information (Byerly & Brodie, 2005; Flanagin & Metzger, 2007). Second, it addresses youth needs for cognitive and social autonomy by inviting them to lead with the issue that matters most to them.

Finally, when youth produce media for council members, peers, and the public at large, they are invited to consider the impact of their words, their facts, and their images. This type of active engagement can also invite more awareness of how factors such as appearance, formatting, and domain name can all be presented as high quality while facts may or may not back up those messages. It also increases the stakes of sharing information, inviting youth to think about the ethical aspects of public dissemination.

For classroom teachers with curricular demands, a semester or year-long intensive research and action cycle (which is typical for youth media and youth-led organizing) is rarely practical. However, some lessons from after-school and out-of-school settings are transferrable to the classroom and can address the questions of experience and salience, reward seeking, and identity work, as well as autonomy and moral authority. In the remainder of this chapter, I offer three practical approaches that teachers can use in their classrooms.

Begin with Engaging Media as a Launching Point for Investigation

One approach to teaching youth to be critical consumers of news is to teach toward a platonic ideal. Teachers may present a topic and then have students analyze one or more articles, videos, cartoons, or podcasts for evidence, authority, bias, missing information, and so on. This approach presents students with a challenge to compare different sources of media and may call their attention to variations in credibility of media. When teachers pick an issue that they believe is relevant to their students (e.g., bullying, school closures, school shootings) this approach is likely even more compelling.

However, if youths let news come to them through social media and pay particular attention to issues introduced through sensational headlines or satire (Clark & Marchi, 2017), then media literacy that begins with rigorous research on a defined topic is not sufficient. Youth need practice with evaluating incidental media and how it shapes their understanding of public issues.

Another approach, then, is to have students track their media use over a period of time, noting what catches their attention (e.g., social media posts, topics brought up in TV shows, statements by celebrities in addition to news media). This approach begins with what students notice and have already paid attention to and then invites them to analyze media in a variety of formats (e.g., clips shared through social media, source material, celebrity statements, mock news, and so on). This approach may be less effective for teaching the skills of conducting formal research, but it can help youth become critical consumers of incidental media.

A different approach might begin with popular media representations of news but with an eye toward deeper investigation of an issue. For example, Clark and Marchi (2017) noted that a participant in their ethnographic study first learned about the Trayvon Martin case through the television show *South Park*. This approach could serve as a starting point for analyzing the different portrayals of the case and other issues of gun control in entertainment media, social media, and news media. It may also serve as a starting point to generate questions about the laws and different perspectives on gun control.

Build Background Knowledge Alongside (Rather Than Before or After) Practicing Skills of Credibility

If expertise on a topic is associated with more attention to credibility cues (Flanagin & Metzger, 2007), then building up background knowledge with teacher-provided readings and class discussion prior to conducting research may be helpful. However, the gains made through this approach will be lost as soon as it is applied to a new topic.

Yet repeated cycles of building background knowledge and researching within a single project and/or over the course of the semester, school year, or school experience could provide youth with greater metacognitive awareness of the relationship between content knowledge and credibility. Being aware of one's own processing of credibility cues and the processing of moving from lesser to greater comfort can help with future media analysis in two ways.

First, awareness of when one is processing credibility cues against formatting and domain name cues can help with knowing when to hold off on coming to conclusions versus feeling confident in one's conclusions. This awareness is particularly important in the context of social media where sharing information is so easy. Self-monitoring can help build more realistic awareness of one's own judgment of credibility.

Second, such practice can build patience in the face of reading about new information. While one concern is that people will share information too easily without evaluating its validity, the opposite concern is giving up easily when it is difficult to tell. When youth have opportunities to repeat the cycle of building up expertise and monitoring their own ease with searching for and evaluating information, they may also learn that expertise can be built with practice.

Engage the Moral Critique of News Media and Discuss the Ethics of Information

Finally, educators can address the challenges of the tendency to be critical of traditional news media and to be drawn to first-person or anecdotal sources by inviting a critical eye for both. Acknowledging the flaws in traditional broadcast and news media organizations' coverage of issues relevant to youth builds trust in the idea that media should be a source of fair and accurate information for all. This ideal is impossible to fully attain, but inviting youth to bring a critical lens and to consider how news media could better suit their needs recognizes their importance.

Additionally, discussing the strengths and limitations of both traditional media and media that is user-generated or from lesser-known sources, can begin a conversation about the ethics of sharing information with others. Think-aloud tasks with a small sample (n = 24) of high school students

(Middaugh, 2018b) found that participants were far less likely to employ credibility cues when deciding what media to share than when explicitly asked to evaluate information. Adolescents' interest in moral critique may also present an opportunity for conversations about their role in sharing media and potentially spreading information.

CONCLUSION

The majority of this chapter has outlined how adolescent and emerging adult development, paired with adolescents' habits of allowing news to come to them through social media, create conditions that may foster attention to fake news. However, the same developmental trends that make adolescents vulnerable are also ones that create opportunities. Adolescents' still-developing brain anatomy means they are more malleable and able to build the connections that support fast, flexible judgments needed for the complexity of online reasoning.

Their hunger for moral clarity and social communication remind us to address some of the flaws of the previous media landscape. Their critique that they are left out of and misrepresented by the news is legitimate and can only be addressed if youth are welcomed into the project of producing and shaping the news media narrative. Youth did not create the fake news problem, nor do they bear primary responsibility, but they can help develop the solution.

REFERENCES

American Press Institute. (2015). How millennials get news: Inside the habits of America's first digital generation. Retrieved from www.americanpressinstitute.org/publications/reports/survey-research/millennials-news/

Barthell, M., Mitchell, A., & Holcomb, J. (2016). Many Americans believe fake news is sowing confusion. *Pew Research Center*. Retrieved from www.journalism.org/2016/12/15/many-americans-believe-fake-news-is-sowing-confusion/

Berry, J., & Sobieraj, S. (2014). *The outrage industry: Political opinion media and the new incivility.* New York, NY: Oxford University Press.

Byerly, G., & Brodie, C. (2005, April). *Internet (and/or institutional) credibility and the user.* Paper presented at the Internet Credibility and the User Symposium, Seattle, WA.

Clark, L. S., & Marchi, R. (2017). *Young people and the future of news: Social media and the rise of connective journalism.* New York, NY: Cambridge University Press.

Cohen, C. J., & Kahne, J. (2018). *Youth participatory politics survey project, 2013.* Ann Arbor, MI: Inter-university Consortium for Political and Social Research. doi.org/10/3886/ICPSR36849.v1

Davis, K. (2013). Young people's digital lives: The impact of interpersonal relationships and digital media use on adolescents' sense of identity. *Computers in Human Behavior, 29,* 2281–2293.

Dwyer, D. B., Harrison, B. J., Yucel, M., Whittle, S., Zalesky, A., Pantelis, C., . . . Fornito, A. (2014). Large-scale brain network dynamics supporting adolescent cognitive control. *Journal of Neuroscience, 34*, 14096–14107.

Erikson, E. H. (1968). *Identity, youth and crisis.* New York, NY: Norton.

Flanagin, A. J., Hocevar, K., & Samahito, S. (2014). Connecting with the user-generated web: How shared social identity impacts online information sharing and evaluation. *Information, Communication, and Society, 17*, 683–694.

Flanagin, A. J., & Metzger, M. J. (2007). The role of site features, user attributes, and information verification behaviors on the perceived credibility of Web-based information. *New Media & Society, 9*, 319–342.

Ginwright, S., & Cammarota, J. (2006). Introduction. In S. Ginwright, P. Noguera, & J. Cammarota (Eds.), *Beyond resistance! Youth activism and community change* (pp. xiii–xxii). New York, NY: Taylor & Francis Group.

Guyer, A., McClure-Tone, E., Shiffrin, N., Pine, D., & Nelson, E. (2009). Probing the neural correlates of anticipated peer evaluation in adolescence. *Child Development, 80*, 1000–1015.

Hobbs, R. (2011). *Digital and media literacy: Connecting culture and classroom.* Thousand Oaks, CA: Corwin Press.

Kahneman, D. (2011). *Thinking, fast and slow.* New York, NY: Farrar, Strauss, & Giroux.

Kirshner, B. (2015). *Youth activism in an era of education inequity.* New York: New York University Press.

Konijn, E. A., Veldhuis, J., Plasier, X. S., Spekman, M., & den Hamer, A. (2015). Adolescent development and psychological mechanisms in interactive media use. In S. Sundar Shyam (Ed.), *The handbook of the psychology of communication technology* (pp. 332–364). Malden, MA: Wiley-Blackwell.

Konijn, E. A., Walma van der Molen, J. H., & van Nes, S. (2009). Emotions bias perceptions of realism in audiovisual media: Why we may take fiction for real. *Discourse Processes, 46*, 309–340.

Kuhn, D. (2009). Adolescent thinking. In R. Lerner & L. Steinberg (Eds.), *Handbook of adolescent psychology* (3rd ed., pp. 152–186). Hoboken, NJ: Wiley.

Lenhart, A. (2015). Teens, social media & technology overview 2015. *Pew Research Center.* Retrieved from www.pewinternet.org/2015/04/09/teens-social-media-technology-2015/

Madden, M., Lenhart, A., Cortesi, S., Gasser, U., Duggan, M., Smith, A., & Beaton, M. (2013). Teens, social media, and privacy: Part I: Teens and social media use. *Pew Research Center.* Retrieved from www.pewinternet.org/2013/05/21/part-1-teens-and-social-media-use/

Martens, H., & Hobbs, R. (2015). How media literacy supports civic engagement in a digital age. *Atlantic Journal of Communication, 23*, 120–137.

McGrew, S., Breakstone, J., Ortega, T., Smith, M., & Wineburg, S. (2018). Can students evaluate online sources? Learning from assessments of civic online reasoning. *Theory & Research in Social Education, 46*, 165–193.

McGrew, S., Ortega, T., Breakstone, J., & Wineburg, S. (2017). The challenge that's bigger than fake news: Civic reasoning in a social media environment. *American Educator, 41*(3), 4–9.

Metzger, M. J., & Flanagin, A. J. (2015). Psychological approaches to credibility assessment online. In S. Sundar Shyam (Ed.), *The handbook of the psychology of communication technology* (pp. 445–466). Malden, MA: Wiley-Blackwell.

Middaugh, E. (2018a). Civic media literacy in a transmedia world: Balancing personal experience, factual accuracy, and emotional appeal as media consumers and circulators. *Journal of Media Literacy Education, 10*(2), 33–52.

Middaugh, E. (2018b). *The impact of exposure to online conflict on youth civic engagement.* Manuscript in preparation.

Middaugh, E., Bowyer B., & Kahne, J. (2017). U Suk! Norms of online political discourse and the implications for adolescent civic development and engagement. *Youth & Society, 49*, 902–922.

NORC at the University of Chicago. (2017, April 21). New survey: Snapchat and Instagram are most popular social media platforms among American teens: Black teens are the most active on social media and messaging apps. Science Daily [Website]. Retrieved from www.sciencedaily.com/releases/2017/04/170421113306.htm

Pierson, D., & Lien, T. (2018). To please users and halt fake news, Facebook makes it harder for real news outlets. *Los Angeles Times.* Retrieved from www.latimes.com/business/la-fi-tn-facebook-shares-20180112-story.html

Robb, M. B.. (2017). *News and America's kids: How young people perceive and are impacted by the news.* San Francisco, CA: Common Sense. Retrieved from www.commonsensemedia.org/sites/default/files/uploads/research/2017_commonsense_newsandamericaskids.pdf

Scola, M. (2018). Twitter purges accounts, and conservatives cry foul. *Politico.* Retrieved from www.politico.com/story/2018/02/21/twitter-purges-accounts-conservatives-357028

Selemon, L. D. (2013). A role for synaptic plasticity in the adolescent development of executive function. *Translational Psychiatry, 3*, 1–9.

Sherman, L. E., Payton, A. A., Hernandez, L. M., Greenfield, P. M., & Dipretto, M. (2016). The power of like in adolescence: Effects of peer influence on neural and behavioral responses to social media. *Psychological Science, 27*, 1027–1035

Smetana, J., & Villalobos, M. (2009). Social cognitive development in adolescence. In R. Lerner & L. Stein (Eds.), *Handbook of adolescent psychology,* (3rd ed., pp. 188–228). New York, NY: Wiley.

Sobieraj, S., & Berry, J. (2011). From incivility to outrage: Political discourse in blogs, talk radio, and cable news. *Political Communication, 28*, 19–41.

Soep, E. (2015). Working the crowd: Youth media interactivity. In J. Flood, S. B. Heath, & D. Lapp (Eds.), *Handbook of research on teaching literacy through the communicative and visual arts* (pp. 271–278). New York, NY: Routledge.

Spies Shapiro, L. A., & Margolin, G. (2014). Growing up wired: Social networking sites and adolescent psychosocial development. *Clinical Child and Family Psychology Review, 17*, 1–18.

Steinberg, L. (2014). *Age of opportunity: Lessons from the new science of adolescence.* New York, NY: Houghton Mifflin Harcourt.

Steinberg, L. (2017). *Adolescence* (11th ed.). New York, NY: McGraw Hill.

Subrahmanyam, K., & Šmahel, D. (2011). *Digital youth: The role of digital media in development*. New York, NY: Springer.
Valentino, N. A., Hutchings, V. L., Banks, A. J., & Davis, A. K. (2008). Is a worried citizen a good citizen? Emotions, political information seeking, and learning via the Internet. *Political Psychology, 29*, 247–273.
Valkenburg, P., & Peter, J. (2013). The differential susceptibility to media effects model. *Journal of Communication, 63*, 221–243. doi:10.1111/jcom.12024

CHAPTER 4

How Students Evaluate Digital News Sources

Sarah McGrew, Joel Breakstone, Teresa Ortega, Mark Smith, and Sam Wineburg

Today's young people inhabit a different information environment from the one that shaped their parents and grandparents. According to an American Press Institute (2015) study, young people encounter the world by checking their Facebook and Twitter feeds instead of reading the local paper or watching the news on television. This change in the way that information is accessed has profound implications for civic life.

Reliable information is to civic health what clean air and clean water are to public health. Healthy democracies need citizens who are able to access, evaluate, and use information to participate in civic life (Hobbs, 2010; Knight Commission on the Information Needs of Communities in a Democracy, 2009; Mihailidis & Thevenin, 2013). The Internet can widen the scope of the stories that are told, democratize access to information, and create new forms of political organization (Kahne, Hodgin, & Eidman-Aadahl, 2016).

Unfortunately, in an environment where so much information travels with relative freedom, misinformation spreads quickly. If youth consume information without the ability to discern its credibility, they risk being deceived. Traditional gatekeepers of information and hallmarks of authority are largely absent online, so it is imperative that students know how to find reliable information on which to base their opinions and decisions (Metzger, 2007; Metzger, Flanagin, & Medders, 2010).

Research on how young people make judgments online suggests that there is reason to be concerned. Communication studies scholars Eszter Hargittai, Lindsay Fullerton, Ericka Menchen-Trevino, and Kristen Thomas (2010) observed more than 100 college students as they searched online for answers to questions for which the Web provided contradictory information.

The disturbing upshot of this work was that students ceded to Google the responsibility for making judgments of credibility. Students believed that a website's position on a page of search results corresponded to its trustworthiness—the higher up, the more trustworthy.

Some students in Hargittai et al.'s (2010) study claimed that they evaluated information by considering a site's authors and their credentials. However, screen-capture data suggested otherwise: No student "actually followed through by verifying either the identification or the qualifications of the authors" (Hargittai et al., 2010, p. 480). Additional studies with students of varying ages have similarly shown that students rarely consider where information came from when deciding whether to trust it (e.g., Barzilai & Zohar, 2012; List, Grossnickle, & Alexander, 2016; Walraven, Brand-Gruwel, & Boshuizen, 2009; Wiley et al., 2009). Instead of evaluating information based on its source, research has found that young people focus on features including a website's relevance to their searching needs, its appearance and familiarity, or how easy it is to navigate (Barzilai & Zohar, 2012; Iding, Crosby, Auernheimer, & Klemm, 2009; Julien & Barker, 2009; Walraven et al., 2009).

These findings indicate that young people are ill-equipped to make social and political decisions based on the information they find online. Given the crucial role that online content plays in civic life, young people need to be prepared to make sense of the misleading, contradictory, and ambiguous information that they will encounter on the Web. In order to help prepare students, teachers need ways to assess students' reasoning about such information. Specifically, they need classroom-ready tools to track progress and facilitate instruction.

ASSESSMENT DEVELOPMENT

Three years ago, we set out to develop assessments of students' *civic online reasoning*—the ability to effectively search for, evaluate, and verify social and political information online (McGrew, Breakstone, Ortega, Smith, & Wineburg, 2018). We use this term in order to highlight the civic aims of this work. It also distinguishes our work from the broader fields of media and digital literacy, which include goals that range from preventing online bullying to creating videos.

We crafted dozens of assessments that directly measure how students evaluate the types of information that stream across their phones: blog posts, Facebook updates, tweets, and Snapchat stories. Designed for middle school, high school, and college, the tasks assess the three main constructs that we identified as the *core competencies* of civic online reasoning. Students must have the dispositions, skills, and knowledge to ask and answer the following questions:

- Who is behind this information?
- What is the evidence?
- What do other sources say?

These competencies emerged from research on how professional fact checkers evaluate online information (Wineburg & McGrew, 2017). Together, they include the ways of thinking that students need to effectively evaluate online information.

Each assessment was put through a rigorous validation process and edited based on the feedback of experienced educators and assessment specialists. We developed easy-to-use scoring guides so that educators could quickly determine whether students possessed the skills needed to make sound judgments. Our task development effort followed practices outlined by assessment experts and mirrored the process we used in developing history assessments (Breakstone, 2014; Pellegrino, Chudowsky, & Glaser, 2001; Schmeiser & Welch, 2006):

1. Identify the construct the task will measure.
2. Draft assessment.
3. Assemble an expert panel to conduct a logical analysis and identify the cognitive demands of the task (Li, Ruiz-Primo, & Shavelson, 2006).
4. Pilot task with students.
5. Analyze student responses to determine whether the task elicits information about student understanding of the targeted constructs and revise the task as needed.
6. Conduct think-aloud interviews with students as they complete the task (American Educational Research Association, American Psychological Association, & National Council on Measurement in Education, 2014; Ericsson & Simon, 1993; Kane, 2006; Taylor & Dionne, 2000).
7. Review think-aloud interview protocols and revise task as needed.

As part of the assessment development process, we created rubrics for each task. Initial drafts of rubrics were based on the type of thinking we hoped to see in student responses. Members of our research team scored initial student responses using the draft rubrics. We analyzed inter-rater agreement and discussed whether the rubrics fully captured the range of thinking displayed in student responses. Based on these deliberations, we revised the rubrics. In some cases, rubrics went through several iterations. Each rubric includes three categories: beginning, emerging, and mastery.

STUDENT RESPONSES

We administered the assessments of civic online reasoning to thousands of students across the country. Their responses were troubling. From middle school through college, students struggled to evaluate online sources. They could not distinguish between news stories and advertisements, had trouble verifying social media accounts, and came up short when asked to determine which groups are behind websites. Responses to these tasks cast doubt on whether students can make the types of informed judgments needed for responsible civic engagement in our current digital landscape.

Who's Behind this Information? Comparing the Source of Facebook Posts

Students often turn to digital platforms for news. But how do they evaluate the information they find there? We explore that question by describing a series of tasks that assess whether students ask—and correctly answer—the questions "Who's behind this information?" and "What's the evidence?" as they evaluate online information.

A paper-and-pencil task for high school students assesses whether students can make accurate judgments about who is behind information in Facebook posts (see Figure 4.1). Specifically, this task assesses students' knowledge of an important symbol on many social media sites—the blue checkmark, which indicates a verified account. Students are asked which of two Facebook posts is a more trustworthy source about Donald Trump's decision to run for president.

Although both posts claim to represent Fox News, only one is verified. Post A is from the verified Fox News account while Post B is from "Fox News the FB Page," an unverified account. Successful students investigate who is behind each post and use the blue check mark to identify the verified account.

One hundred sixty students at four different high schools completed the final version of this task. The results suggest that many students did not prioritize comparing the sources of each post and are not familiar with key social media conventions. Twenty-six percent of students constructed "mastery" responses. These students recognized and explained the significance of the blue check mark and used it to argue that Post A was more reliable because it was the authentic Fox News account. As one student wrote:

> As you can see, there is a checkmark beside the Facebook name "Fox News." That lets you know that it is the real Fox News, unlike the other. Anyone can make a fake account about Fox News, but the check mark next to the username lets you know they are the real deal.

Nine percent of students wrote responses that were scored as "emerging." These students selected Post A as the more trustworthy source and provided partial explanations. They either identified the blue checkmark but did not explain its significance or identified Post A as coming from the "real" Fox News but did not explain how they knew. For example, one

Figure 4.1. The "News on Facebook" Task

Facebook Post A / Facebook Post B (circle one) is a more trustworthy source about Donald Trump's decision to run for president because ....

....

....

....

student wrote, "Post A is more reliable because it is from a reliable and official news website."

Sixty-five percent of student responses fell into the "beginning" category. Responses in this category were split in their selection of Post A or Post B as the more trustworthy source; however, all answers were based on incorrect or irrelevant reasoning about the posts. About half of the students in the "beginning" category focused on comparing the content of the posts and argued that Post B was more trustworthy because it included a supposed tweet from Donald Trump announcing his candidacy. As one student explained, Post B was more trustworthy "because it shows that Donald Trump himself said that he's running for president on his social media website."

These results demonstrate that students may focus more on the content of social media posts than on their sources. Instead of carefully comparing the sources of the posts and looking for markers of authenticity, many students were duped by the concocted tweet purportedly authored by Trump and used it as the basis to decide which post was more trustworthy.

What's the Evidence? Evaluating Evidence in a Tweet

Another task assesses whether students can effectively evaluate the evidence provided for a claim. Social media is filled with political claims followed by links to stories that supposedly provide support. Often, social media users do not take the time to even open and read those linked stories before

Figure 4.2. The "Claims on Twitter" Task (Students began this task in the Google Form shown on the left and, when they clicked the link provided in the form, were led to the tweet on the right)

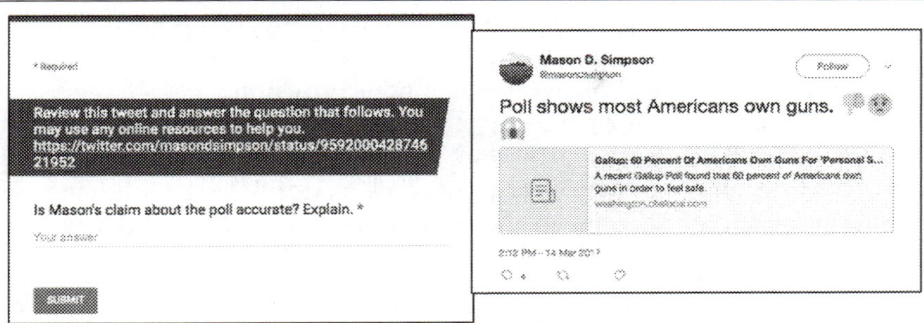

liking, commenting, or sharing the original post on their social media feeds (Gabielkov, Ramachandran, Chaintreau, & Legout, 2016). Would students actually visit the linked article to evaluate the story for themselves, or would they accept the tweet's framing of the article and base their judgment of the claim on other factors?

This task is delivered via Google Forms and provides students a link to a tweet by a Twitter user named Mason D. Simpson (see Figure 4.2). In the tweet Simpson claims, "Poll shows that most Americans own guns" followed by three emojis: a thumbs down, a frowning face, and a horrified face. The tweet links to an article from a Washington, DC–based CBS local news station whose headline (as it is visible in the Twitter preview) reads "Gallup: 60 Percent of Americans Own Guns for 'Personal S…'" The task instructs students that they can use any online resources to answer the question: Is Mason [Simpson]'s claim about the poll accurate? Explain.

Although Simpson claimed that the poll shows that most Americans own guns and the article preview provided by Twitter suggests the same, clicking on the link to read the full article reveals a different picture. In fact, the article reports on a poll of just 309 American *gun owners*, 60% of whom said they own a gun for reasons related to personal safety. In order to successfully complete this task, students need to open the link, read at least the first two sentences of the article, and evaluate Simpson's claim based on what they learn.

One hundred eighty-seven students at three different high schools completed the final version of this task. Students struggled to effectively evaluate Simpson's claim. Eighty percent of student responses fell into the "beginning" category of our rubric. Although these students were divided on whether Simpson's claim was accurate or inaccurate, they all provided incorrect or irrelevant reasoning.

Thirty percent of students argued that Simpson's claim was accurate. Many of these students based their responses on their personal experiences or opinions. For example, one student wrote, "I think it's pretty accurate as my father and I myself own guns so I believe most Americans do." A student with a different opinion about guns wrote, "Yes, there's a lot of people who want AK-47 to 'protect' themselves in a home invasion."

Forty-eight percent of students argued that Simpson's claim was inaccurate but used incorrect or irrelevant reasoning. These responses were also scored as "beginning." Many of these students took issue with Simpson's claim because they questioned the Gallup poll on which it was based. As one student argued,

> No, because that poll could easily be biased as it is very very hard to take an accurate poll of all American citizens. I do not personally think it is possible to get an even somewhat accurate result of how many people own guns.

This student objected to the fact that a poll was conducted (and revealed misconceptions about polling) instead of noting the difference between the topic of the poll and the substance of Simpson's claim. Other students who wrote "beginning" responses that questioned Simpson's claim provided inaccurate or unsourced data about how many Americans own guns or argued that 60% is not, as Simpson claimed, "most" Americans.

Just 13% of students wrote "mastery" responses. These students questioned Simpson's claim and explained the difference between his position and the data from the linked article. One student explained:

> No. A quick read of the article shows that the researchers surveyed gun owning Americans and that 60% of them responded that the reason that they own a gun is to protect themselves. In other words, 60% of gun owning Americans have a gun in order to attain personal safety. No one who was polled didn't own a gun, so saying most Americans own guns is very misleading.

This response shows that this student visited the linked article, scanned the story, and then evaluated Simpson's claim based on what she read.

Asked to evaluate a claim on Twitter, most students struggled to effectively critique the evidence provided to back it up. Responses suggest that many students did not follow the hyperlink to the news report in order to determine if it supported the poster's claim. Instead, most students offered personal opinions about gun ownership or irrelevant critiques of polling methods. These results highlight the need to explicitly teach students to check whether linked articles support posted claims before they accept them, let alone like, comment, or share.

Who's Behind This Information and What's the Evidence? Analyzing a YouTube Video

Students also turn to video sharing sites like YouTube for news about the world. Videos are powerful, popular, and easy to make. Compelling footage and authoritative narration may tempt students to trust such videos without stopping to ask, "Who is behind this information?" and "What is the evidence?" In order to effectively evaluate a video, students need to investigate who made it, who posted it, and whether the video provides reliable evidence for the claims it makes.

An online task for high school students assesses whether students ask these questions about a short video that makes a contentious claim. The video shows a series of excerpts from a speech by Shirley Sherrod, who was an official from the U.S. Department of Agriculture (USDA) at the time. Selective editing made it seem as though Sherrod described an instance in which she discriminated against a farmer on the basis of his race while working for the government. After the video went viral, Sherrod was fired by the USDA.

In the days following Sherrod's dismissal, additional information emerged. The video had been created by a conservative activist seeking to discredit President Barack Obama's administration, which had appointed Sherrod. An unedited version of Sherrod's speech was released, which made it clear that the first video was misleading, and the officials who fired Sherrod apologized.

In this Google Forms task (see Figure 4.3), students are provided with the name of the person who posted the video (Larry O'Connor) and Sherrod's position in the Department of Agriculture. They are also told that the video shows only parts of her 45-minute speech. Students watch the 2½-minute video clip embedded in the form and then answer this question: This video claims that Sherrod discriminated against a farmer due to his race. Why might you not trust this video?

We administered the final version of this task to 136 students at three different high schools. Even though the question asked them directly why the video might *not* be trustworthy, students struggled to identify its most problematic elements. Just 20% of students wrote "mastery" responses. These students reasoned effectively about the video's creator, considered the impact of selective editing, and provided complete explanations about why those elements made the video untrustworthy. For example, one student argued:

> The video seems to have been trimmed to particular parts. Whether or not this was Sherrod's true message, the video editor could have bent her words to his will and easily warped her message. I would be more willing to believe the video had I have been given context as well as Shirley Sherrod's full speech in order to understand her whole narrative given to the NAACP that day.

Figure 4.3. The "Claims on YouTube" Task

Watch the video below and answer the question that follows.

This video was uploaded by YouTube user Larry O'Connor on July 18, 2010. The video shows parts of a forty-five-minute speech Shirley Sherrod delivered in March 2010. At the time of the speech, Sherrod was Georgia State Director of Rural Development for the United States Department of Agriculture.

This video claims that Sherrod discriminated against a farmer due to his race. Why might you not trust this video? *

Your answer

SUBMIT

Fifty-five percent of students wrote "beginning" responses. These students provided a wide range of irrelevant reasons for distrusting the video. For example, students discounted the video based on its poor audio quality or the fact that Sherrod did not provide enough "evidence" in her story. Other "beginning" responses accepted the video's argument that Sherrod was racist and, based on her bias, maintained that she was not a trustworthy source.

Still other students argued about whether the situation that Sherrod described in the video, in which she hesitated to help a White farmer in danger of losing his farm, was truly an example of racism. For example, one student wrote,

> I wouldn't trust this video because it failed to give good reliable evidence on why or how she discriminates against people of a different race. They gave a situation where she didn't help a white man as much as she could have, but that isn't really discrimination.

These students did not question the video's trustworthiness. Instead, they took it at face value and argued about the conclusions drawn based on it.

Finally, 24% of responses were in the "emerging" category. These students were on the right track but either did not provide enough explanation or included additional incorrect or irrelevant reasoning. For example, one student wrote, "It doesn't show her whole speech so it's not that trustworthy." Although this statement is technically correct, it is so general that it could be made about many videos.

Although students spend a great deal of time on sites like YouTube, student responses to this task suggest that they have a lot to learn about how to effectively evaluate the content on these sites. Instead of analyzing the video of Sherrod based on its partisan source and its selective editing, students made arguments based on less important features of the video (e.g., its production quality) or engaged with its argument. These students may be led astray by videos unless they learn more effective evaluation strategies.

HOW CAN WE HELP STUDENTS DO BETTER?

Identifying Effective Online Evaluation Strategies

Students are often unprepared to investigate the credibility of digital information. In order to help them, we recognized the need to identify effective online evaluation strategies and engaged in an effort to map expertise in the evaluation of digital sources. The undertaking has been more complicated than we expected because it was a challenge to determine who, exactly, qualifies as an expert.

Given our prior research on historical reading (Wineburg, 1991, 1998), we turned first to historians, people who evaluate sources for a living. We asked a group of 10 historians to complete a series of web-based tasks, such as evaluating the credibility of an unfamiliar website. We recorded their computer screens and their narrations of what they were doing as they navigated the web. We were taken aback by the difficulty these historians had in navigating *digital* sources—difficulties that held constant even as historians' ages and areas of expertise varied. It turned out that historians were only slightly better than a group of Stanford undergraduates (n = 25) who completed the same hour-long set of tasks (Wineburg & McGrew, 2017).

Another group performed much better. We asked 10 professional fact checkers from some of the nation's leading publications to complete the same set of tasks. We discovered that fact checkers approach unfamiliar digital information differently than other users. For example, they prioritized investigating the sources of the websites they were asked to evaluate. Rather than scrolling up and down to read the content of the page, fact checkers *read laterally:* they left the original site within seconds and opened up new browser tabs to examine what other sites said about the original source. Only after they had a sense of whether the source was reliable did they return to the original site, better oriented to the information at hand. Fact checkers read less than other groups but learned more.

In a world where we are deluged by digital information, we need effective strategies for making informed decisions on civic issues. The questions about online information that fact checkers prioritized and their strategies for investigating those questions provide a potential path forward. How might we teach these dispositions and strategies in classrooms?

New Instructional Approaches

The tasks we have developed (available at sheg.stanford.edu) are not only assessments; they can also be used as instructional tools. Each assessment can serve as the beginning of a broader lesson. Moreover, teachers do not have to rework their entire curricula to teach online reasoning. Instead, they can integrate it in smaller pieces.

Across the course of a school year, teachers could introduce the core competencies (Who's behind this information? What's the evidence? and What do other sources say?) and teach students strategies for investigating each question. Consider how each of the tasks described in this chapter could be used as the basis for a lesson about civic online reasoning.

In order to introduce the importance of asking "Who is behind this information?" a teacher could ask students to complete the assessment about Trump's announcement to run for president. Afterwards, students could work in pairs to brainstorm all of the possible factors to take into account to determine which post is more trustworthy (e.g., the name of the sources, the presence of the blue checkmark, the date each was posted, and so on).

The teacher could then instruct students to discuss and select the most important feature to use in determining whether the source is trustworthy and lead a discussion on students' decisions. Over the course of the discussion, the teacher could help students understand why the posts should be judged primarily based on where they came from—and how the blue checkmark is a useful guide. In this way, the teacher could address misconceptions students might have about the posts, including that one is more trustworthy because it includes "evidence" from Trump himself in the form of a tweet.

Similarly, a teacher could use the assessment with the tweet from Mason D. Simpson about gun ownership to introduce the importance of asking "What is the evidence?" After students complete the task, the teacher could raise the importance of explicitly verifying evidence on social media and lead the class in brainstorming verification strategies. For example, students could start by investigating Simpson's Twitter account, asking whether the person responsible for the account is a reliable source of information on gun ownership.

Next, they could click on the link to the news story in the tweet to evaluate both the source of the article and the evidence it provides. Finally, students could attempt to prove or disprove Simpson's claim with an unrelated and reliable source. Students could then revise their answers to the original task and reflect on why their answers changed.

The Sherrod video task provides an opportunity to address strategies for evaluating an online video. Because the task is complex, teachers might choose to model their approach to evaluating the video for students after the class has watched the edited video together.

Through modeling, the teacher could demonstrate that while it may be tempting for students to simply accept what they see in videos as the truth, it is imperative that they question where the information comes from and whether it has been taken out of context. While discussing these questions, the teacher could demonstrate the ways in which the video falls short of providing evidence for the claim it makes. In order to extend the lesson about evaluating video sources and evidence, the teacher could show students portions of the unedited video of Sherrod's speech and discuss how the edited video distorts Sherrod's message.

Teaching students to be careful consumers of online information will require the efforts of teachers from all subject areas. Students will benefit most if they have varied experiences evaluating information throughout the school day. For example, science teachers could have students evaluate websites created by climate change deniers; English teachers could help students recognize and respond to online propaganda; math teachers could show students how to identify deceitful uses of polling data and statistics; social studies teachers could help students distinguish between articles that have gone through rigorous peer review and pseudoscholarly arguments based on footnotes to dubious sources.

Finally, we have to recognize that the challenge goes beyond students. Although our tasks focused on assessing students' abilities to evaluate online information, adults also need support in developing strategies for evaluating digital content, and teachers will require professional development in this area. Teachers also need instruction in how to incorporate these new digital strategies into their classrooms, models for what such integration could look like, and time to plan ways to teach online reasoning.

REFERENCES

American Educational Research Association (AERA), American Psychological Association (APA), & National Council on Measurement in Education (NCMW). (2014). *Standards for educational and psychological testing*. Washington, DC: American Educational Research Association.

American Press Institute. (2015). *How millennials get news: Inside the habits of America's first digital generation*. Retrieved from www.americanpressinstitute.org/publications/reports/survey-research/millennials-news/

Barzilai, S., & Zohar, A. (2012). Epistemic thinking in action: Evaluating and integrating online sources. *Cognition and Instruction, 30*, 39–85.

Breakstone, J. (2014). Try, try, try again: The process of designing new history assessments. *Theory & Research in Social Education, 42*, 453–485.

Ericsson, K. A., & Simon, H. A. (1993). *Protocol analysis: Verbal reports as data* (Rev. ed.). Cambridge, MA: Massachusetts Institute of Technology Press.

Gabielkov, M., Ramachandran, A., Chaintreau, A., & Legout, A. (2016, June). *Social clicks: What and who gets read on Twitter?* Paper presented at the ACM SIGMETRICS Conference, Antibes Juan-les-Pins, France.

Hargittai, E., Fullerton, L., Menchen-Trevino, E., & Thomas, K. Y. (2010). Trust online: Young adults' evaluation of Web content. *International Journal of Communication, 4*, 468–494.

Hobbs, R. (2010). *Digital and media literacy: A plan of action*. Washington, DC: Aspen Institute. Retrieved from www.aspeninstitute.org/publications/digital-media-literacy-plan-action-2/

Iding, M. K., Crosby, M. E., Auernheimer, B., & Klemm, E. B. (2009). Web site credibility: Why do people believe what they believe? *Instructional Science, 37*, 43–63.

Julien, H., & Barker, S. (2009). How high school students find and evaluate scientific information: A basis for information literacy skills development. *Library & Information Science Research, 31*, 12–17.

Kahne, J., Hodgin, E., & Eidman-Aadahl, E. (2016). Redesigning civic education for the digital age: Participatory politics and the pursuit of democratic engagement. *Theory & Research in Social Education, 44*, 1–35.

Kane, M. T. (2006). Validation. In R. L. Brennan (Ed.), *Educational measurement* (4th ed., pp. 17–64). Westport, CT: Praeger.

Knight Commission on the Information Needs of Communities in a Democracy. (2009). *Informing communities: Sustaining democracy in the digital age*. Washington, DC: Aspen Institute. Retrieved from knightfoundation.org/reports/informing-communities-sustaining-democracy-digital

Li, M., Ruiz-Primo, M., & Shavelson, R. (2006). Towards a science achievement framework: The case of TIMSS 1999. In S. Howie & T. Plomp (Eds.), *Contexts of learning mathematics and science: Lessons learned from TIMSS* (pp. 291–311). London, United Kingdom: Routledge.

List, A., Grossnickle, E. M., & Alexander, P. A. (2016). Undergraduate students' justifications for source selection in a digital academic context. *Journal of Educational Computing Research, 54,* 22–61.

McGrew, S., Breakstone, J., Ortega, T., Smith, M., & Wineburg, S. (2018). Can students evaluate online sources? Learning from assessments of civic online reasoning. *Theory & Research in Social Education, 46,* 165–193.

Metzger, M. J. (2007). Making sense of credibility on the web: Models for evaluating online information and recommendations for future research. *Journal of the American Society for Information Science and Technology*, *58*, 2078–2091.

Metzger, M. J., Flanagin, A. J., & Medders, R. B. (2010). Social and heuristic approaches to credibility evaluation online. *Journal of Communication*, *60*, 413–439.

Mihailidis, P., & Thevenin, B. (2013). Media literacy as a core competency for engaged citizenship in participatory democracy. *American Behavioral Scientist*, *57*, 1611–1622.

Pellegrino, J. W., Chudowsky, N., & Glaser, R. (2001). *Knowing what students know.* Washington, DC: National Academies Press.

Schmeiser, C. B., & Welch, C. J. (2006). Test development. In R. L. Brennan (Ed.), *Educational measurement* (4th ed., pp. 307–354). Westport, CT: Praeger.

Taylor, K. L., & Dionne, J. (2000). Accessing problem-solving strategy knowledge: The complementary use of concurrent verbal protocols and retrospective debriefing. *Journal of Educational Psychology*, *92*, 413–425.

Walraven, A., Brand-Gruwel, S., & Boshuizen, H. (2009). How students evaluate information and sources when searching the World Wide Web for information. *Computers & Education, 52*, 234–246.

Wiley, J., Goldman, S. R., Graesser, A. C., Sanchez, C. A., Ash, I. K., & Hemmerich, J. A. (2009). Source evaluation, comprehension, and learning in Internet science inquiry tasks. *American Educational Research Journal, 46,* 1060–1106.

Wineburg, S. (1991). Historical problem solving: A study of the cognitive processes used in the evaluation of documentary and pictorial evidence. *Journal of Educational Psychology, 83*, 73–87.

Wineburg, S. (1998). Reading Abraham Lincoln: An expert/expert study in the interpretation of historical texts. *Cognitive Science, 22*, 319–346.

Wineburg, S., & McGrew, S. (2017). Lateral reading: Reading less and learning more when evaluating digital information (Stanford History Education Group Working Paper No. 2017-A1). Retrieved from ssrn.com/abstract=3048994

CHAPTER 5

Teaching in the Twilight Zone of Misinformation, Disinformation, Alternative Facts, and Fake News

Avner Segall, Margaret Smith Crocco, Anne-Lise Halvorsen, and Rebecca Jacobsen

An urgent and lively discussion has arisen, both in academia and beyond, about the crisis of fake news and our "post-truth" society. Reflecting the prevalence of this condition, Oxford Dictionaries declared *post-truth* as its word of 2016, defining it as the state of affairs when "objective facts are less influential in shaping public opinion than appeals to emotion and personal belief" (para. 1). *Fake news* consists of deliberate misinformation or disinformation disseminated with the intent to mislead readers about a topic or issue. The label has also been used as an "accusation leveled at facts one doesn't like" (Young, 2017, p. 353).

According to Angie Drobnic Holan (2016), the editor of *PolitiFact*, fake news is "the boldest sign of a post-truth society. When we can't agree on basic facts—or even that there are such things as facts," she asks, "how do we talk to each other?" (para. 12). Indeed, much of the talking in our post-truth, partisan society has been *at* each other rather than *to* or *with* each other.

This divisive discourse has been driven, in part, by the ubiquity of politically motivated untruths, half-truths, misinformation, and fake news—what used to be called "lies"—and their acceptance by large portions of the population as true. The widespread circulation of such purposeful disinformation has broken down the boundaries between real and fake news (Kavanagh & Rich, 2018) and undermined standards of evidence and verification. Of even greater concern, perhaps, is the confirmation by social scientists that fake news circulates faster and more widely than real news (Lazer et al., 2018).

Although returning to a civic discourse governed by verified truths and facts is important and necessary, this chapter argues that a better understanding is needed about what underlies and motivates people to gravitate toward untruths, how those circulate, and what impact they have within civic discourse. In this chapter we draw on data from a high school classroom deliberation on U.S. immigration policy that occurred in the period leading to and following the 2016 presidential election to highlight the ways in which fake news, confirmation bias, and motivated reasoning circulate and advance particular ideological and ethical positions.

Our use of the term *fake news* may appear problematic since the subjects of this study—high school students—are not in positions of power to manufacture fake news and disseminate it widely. We use the term more broadly, referring to two aspects prevalent in the deliberation:

- Misinformation/disinformation that students circulated during the deliberation
- Verified evidence that students did not like and thus treated as fake news

DEFINING, UNDERSTANDING, AND RESPONDING TO THE CRISIS

Organizations such as *PolitiFact* and *FactCheck.org* have been scrutinizing news and verifying claims made by politicians for decades. Meanwhile, academics have been sounding the alarm bells about the public's inability to differentiate between what is false and what is true, especially as Internet news outlets have proliferated and become significant sources of information for some people, often replacing traditional journalistic resources such as major newspapers.

Researchers associated with the Stanford History Education Group (Breakstone, McGrew, Smith, Ortega, & Wineburg, 2018; McGrew, Breakstone, Ortega, Smith, & Wineburg, 2018) examined students' ability to detect bias and falsehoods in digital messages. They found that despite students' fluency with social media, many were unable to detect partisanship in media content and lacked skills necessary to verify digital information—an essential component of news literacy. Another study by Wineburg and McGrew (2017) determined that historians, like university undergraduates, also have difficulty differentiating fake news from real news online. Similar results have been demonstrated regarding the broader population (e.g., Kruglanski, 2017; Silverman & Singer-Vine, 2016).

Although some schools still ignore the issue of fake news and its effects, others—alarmed by students' fallibility in differentiating truth from falsehood—have stressed fact-checking procedures in classrooms. On National Public Radio, Cory Turner and Kat Lonsdorf (2016) have reported some teachers using the News Literacy Project's Checkology Virtual Classroom to equip students with tools to interpret information, navigate the challenges of the contemporary information landscape, and "learn how to decide what news and information to trust, share and act on" (The News Literacy Project, 2018, para. 2).

As recent research indicates, however, such efforts alone do not necessarily address (or resolve) the complex relationships among facts, evidence, and people's perceptions of what is true. Evidence or facts, in and of themselves, are not an inherent remedy for fake news. Cognitive filters, logical fallacies, poor reasoning skills, inadequate access to all the facts, belief in things that are not true, not knowing what you do not know—all these and other challenges to critical thinking interfere with people's ability to draw conclusions that are well-grounded (Levitan, 2016). Yet the problems of reasoning go beyond such issues.

As Marshall Alcorn (2013), a faculty member of the Washington Center of Psychoanalysis, noted, people "do not abandon beliefs called into question by factual information; they resist modes of reason that threaten their identities" (p. 46). Political scientists Brendan Nyhan and Jason Reifler (2010) argued that, more often than not, corrections to misperceptions fail to change minds; instead, they may actually result in a "backfire" or "boomerang" effect (Garrett, 2017, p. 49) whereby initial views are often further entrenched rather than abandoned in the face of additional information (Flynn, Nyhan, & Reifler, 2016; Sharot, 2017).

The inability of facts, as true and verified as they may be, to persuade and change minds, is partly due to what is called "motivated reasoning" (Kahne & Bowyer, 2017) or "confirmation bias." Both help explain why students (and the public more broadly), regardless of ideology, might gravitate toward fake news and accept it as true (Bowyer & Kahne, 2017).

Motivated reasoning and *confirmation bias* are mechanisms that work both to defend oneself psychologically by affirming one's existing views about the world and to ignore those other facts that might trouble such views. Motivated reasoning inclines individuals toward information—or facts—that appeals to their emotions, beliefs, and worldview. In other words, even facts "that make little sense or collapse under scrutiny are often accepted as true when they tell us what we want to hear" (Burmila, 2017, para. 12). While these phenomena propel us to accept and embrace knowledge we desire, they also, and simultaneously, involve a particular form of ignorance.

Ignorance, in this case, to use Shoshana Felman's (1982) psychoanalytic definition of the term, is not simply a lack of knowledge (missing knowledge) but rather an active desire to ignore knowledge that, even if it is true, may trouble a person because it does not fit into an already existing view of the world. This form of ignorance is a desire to avoid what makes individuals uncomfortable or challenges or undermines their sense of self, values, or worldview (Garrett, 2017; Lorch, 2017; Sharot, 2017).

These processes apply to the classroom and to the learning and lack of learning that goes on there. Regardless of how many facts and how much evidence a teacher presents or how many fact-checking exercises students engage in, motivated reasoning and confirmation bias will play a role in the process of learning and not learning.

The description of classroom deliberations in three social studies classrooms discussed here begins to get at these dynamics. The data are drawn from a larger study examining students' understanding about, and use of, evidence in public policy deliberations. The description that follows first explores several broader issues pertaining to students' use of evidence in public policy decision making and then analyzes an extended excerpt from one of the classroom deliberations on immigration policy.

FAKE NEWS, MOTIVATED REASONING, AND CONFIRMATION BIAS IN ACTION: A PORTRAIT

Data presented are drawn from a multiphase, year-long, mixed-methods study conducted in four social studies classrooms in three high schools in the Midwest. The study, conducted in 2016 during the period leading to and following the presidential election, explored students' understanding about, and use of, evidence in three contexts:

- In the abstract
- In the context of a particular historical case (*Brown v. Board of Education*, 1954)
- During two classroom deliberations—one on immigration, the other on Internet privacy

The first two phases of the study, the ones involving students' thinking about evidence in the abstract and in the context of the *Brown* case, included data from 10 focal students in each of the three classes. One-on-one interviews with all 30 focal students were conducted following each activity. The third phase of the study comprised two whole-class deliberations on two public policy issues. We use here the definition of *deliberation* given by Parker and Hess (2001), who call deliberation a form of discussion "that is aimed at reaching a decision at an action plan that will resolve a problem that a 'we' faces" (p. 282).

The deliberations were videotaped and transcribed. Once again, one-on-one interviews were conducted with all the focal students following each deliberation.[1] For the purpose of this chapter, data are drawn from the deliberation on immigration in Glendale, one of the three schools studied. We use this particular deliberation since it presents the broadest range of student perspectives on immigration among the three schools studied.

Glendale High School is located in a middle-class, mostly White, small midwestern town situated close to a postindustrial urban center. The student body was comprised of 74% White students and 26% students of color (15% African American, 4% Hispanic, 3% Asian, and 3% multiracial). Twenty-seven percent of the students were eligible for free or reduced-price lunch. The class observed had no immigrants, although parents of at least four students came to the United States from the Middle East on professional visas, as was disclosed by students during the deliberation.

Students raised an impressive number of issues related to immigration, including federal policy, economics, safety, human value (and values) and the pragmatics of living. Students came at these issues using different lenses, ideologies, and epistemologies in locating (or avoiding) political, social, and moral questions, as well as attempting to resolve them. Overall, students exemplified the clash of ideologies across the political divide and a wide range of perspectives about politics, economics, and security, all accompanied by prominent U.S. narratives ranging from nativism, protectionism, and isolationism, on the one hand, to a global sense of responsibility underlined by an ethics of care, compassion, and concern for others beyond one's own national borders, on the other.

Broad consensus emerged among the students that current immigration policies were broken and need fixing. There was less agreement, however, as to what the actual "problem" of immigration entailed and what "fixing the problem" might include. Students were evenly split between those who wished to restrict immigration (particularly illegal immigration) and those who called for more open borders.

The first group of students argued in favor of restricting immigration, defending their position by asserting that undocumented immigrants take American jobs, do not contribute to the economy, burden the social safety net, and pose a threat to safety and national security. The second group of students retorted that undocumented immigrants are unnecessarily put in situations that do not afford them the dignity they deserve.

The problems raised by the first group, students in the second group suggested, are not with the immigrants themselves but with a U.S. system that discriminates against them, denies them opportunities for success, and then blames them for their lot, much like it does with poor Americans. Immigrants, the second group suggested, should not be considered a burden but contributing members of society who deserve compassion and care.

The two excerpts below from the class deliberation (which are abbreviated and compressed for the purpose of this chapter) illustrate how some of the students' utterances are manifestations of fake news, confirmation bias, and motivated reasoning. The use of these cognitive maneuvers shows how they get deployed to sustain particular positions and ignore others, as well as to advance specific societal narratives on both sides of the political aisle about who Americans are and what America ought to be.

Students' utterances also shed light on how language gets mobilized during classroom deliberations, how students use it to situate themselves and their ideas, and what values, dispositions, and political, social, and ethical positioning that language invokes and makes possible. This snapshot of classroom deliberation provides a glimpse of the ways in which fake news enters the life of a classroom and contributes to the dynamics of motivated reasoning.

The following excerpt is not followed by a fine-grained discourse analysis but rather by a critical exploration of utterances and their relation to broader societal narratives about immigration, social responsibility, ethics, and the desirable direction of U.S. public policy. Since much of the exploration concerns facts and the ways in which they were mobilized in the deliberation, some background is needed regarding the setup for the deliberation.

Prior to the deliberation, the research team provided the teacher with a set of evidence packets, eight pages in length, with a variety of evidentiary resources representing different political perspectives on the immigration issue. The packets included evidence in the form of statistical data, research, expert judgment, personal experiences, secondhand accounts or anecdotes, examples, and laws or policies. Students were instructed to use the evidence resources to support one of three positions regarding immigration policy.[2]

Besides being asked to distribute and review these packets, we provided the teacher with no explicit directions for how to conduct the deliberation. Since this was the first deliberation to be conducted by this teacher in this classroom, the teacher weighed the advantages and disadvantages of several deliberation models in consideration of the particular context of the classroom.

Ultimately, the teacher decided to assume a hands-off approach, whereby the teacher would begin class by explaining the rules for the deliberation and pose the three policy options to the students and then mostly stay out of the way, allowing students to deliberate among themselves. In a few instances, the teacher took on the role of "devil's advocate," posing questions to the class that attempted to bring out other voices. The teacher also tracked student participation and encouraged, in a few instances, students who had been silent to join the deliberation.

The day before the deliberation, the teacher reviewed the evidence packet with the students in order to answer questions and clear up any confusion. Students were instructed to go over the packet again for homework to prepare for their position-taking the next day. With the exception of one student (Natalie, who invoked the fact that undocumented immigrants contribute $11.84 billion in state and local taxes each year, a fact included in the packet), little reference to the evidence packet was made during the deliberation itself.

Instead, students repeatedly invoked other facts (or "facts") assembled from elsewhere—from the Internet, personal experience, or hearsay. The vetted facts (from credible sources) included in the packet played little role in students' arguments, almost as if students were never exposed to them or that they did not matter in their minds when discussing a public issue.

STUDENTS TALKING IMMIGRATION POLICY: FACT AS FICTION/FICTION AS FACT

The deliberation began with Hamid, a male of Middle Eastern heritage whose parents came to the United States many years ago on a professional visa. Hamid suggested that "we should welcome anyone who wants to come into our country. Obviously, there's an issue with illegal immigration, but giving them a chance to come here legally is going to be better for everyone."

Kevin, a White male and a strong proponent of stricter immigration policy, entered the deliberation a minute or two later, saying,

> There is a national security threat [from] people coming from Mexico. Ninety-seven percent of immigrants who come across the Mexican border come across it illegally. Of those, 23% committed some kind of traffic violation; another 23% committed some kind of drug-related violation; another 12% committed some kind of either sexual assault, larceny, or burglary crime. That's the majority of people who are coming across the border.

The exchange continued:

> *Latisha* (African American female): Is it a morality issue or is it more of a necessity? Because they come into here with basically nothing. So, if they have nothing, they are going to do anything they can to get something, which may involve criminal activity.
>
> *Kevin:* I don't think *that's* the problem. A lot of people are poor in the world right now. . . . I mean, you always see commercials of starving people, say in Africa. But the thing is, those people were starving when my grandpa was a kid, they were starving when my dad was a kid, and they were starving when I was a kid to now. You see, you're never going to make those people rich by coming into the country. And the economic effects of those coming into the country are pretty bad, too.
>
> *Latisha:* Yet, if they want to come into this country, why should we stop them?
>
> *Kevin:* Well, there are moral and economic issues that are around it. For one, taxpayers are taking the burden for that. See, the average illegal immigrant coming into the country makes only about $25,000 a year, but they only pay $10,000 in taxes. So, there's a deficit of $14,000 that the government needs to cover for each of those families. Cumulatively, that would be about $52 million for all the people that are in there. And also, because they are not making so much income they also need support. Education alone is $52

million for all the total, for all the illegal immigrant groups in [the] country.

Natalie (White female): I would like to point out that even though they are getting federal money they are also, all together, bringing in \$11.84 billion in state and local taxes and, if your argument would be valid in all cases, that means that all poor people shouldn't be supported because they aren't making a substantial amount of income to even out what the federal government is giving them.

Scott (White male) [ignoring Natalie's comment and referring back to Kevin's statement]: So, what I'm hearing from you is that the number of illegal immigrants coming in are more of a burden than they are a benefit to America, to our economy. Is that right?

Kevin [avoiding Scott's question in order to respond to Natalie]: Well, the difference between what you said and illegal immigrants is that they're illegal. They came into the country illegally; they are collecting a total of \$18 billion dollars that the taxpayers need to pay. If they're only putting back into the economy \$11.84 billion, that's nothing. That's dismal compared to what some native, or legal, taxpayer would be paying.

The above exchange might seem familiar in that its essence is commonly reflected in multiple discussions on immigration in the media and in living rooms across the country. Of interest here, however, is not only the substance of the deliberation but also the manner in which particular untruths, motivated reasoning, and confirmation bias coincide to produce specific narratives that serve as justification for particular ideological and ethical stances.

For example, Kevin uses his time to inundate his classmates with a barrage of statistics to demonstrate the criminality of undocumented immigrants coming across the Mexican border and the danger they pose to national security. It is worth pausing for a moment to comment on his technique. Bombarding others with statistics—whether correct or not—is most often done in the hope that more data would bolster one's case, hoping that the avalanche of information will either cover up what the argument lacks or, alternatively, intimidate or numb the audience so they do not question these data.

Drawing on numbers and simple math is also an important persuasive technique given our cultural norms about "hard data" and numbers as truth (Porter, 1996). After all, the saying goes, "You can't argue with the numbers!" As the remainder of the deliberation illustrates, Kevin's tactic worked. His fellow students did not challenge his statistics nor the conclusions they advanced.

In a postdeliberation interview with Kevin, he said he found those statistics on the Internet. Our quick search revealed that they were from the

Heritage Foundation website (Von Spakovsky & Strobl, 2017), an influential conservative think tank. Kevin went to the site in order to, as he indicated later in the interview, substantiate and bolster, as confirmation bias would invite him to do, the position about immigration that he held prior to the deliberation.

Yet Kevin did not simply incorporate the data he found. He took it one step further, amending the data to make the statistics more compelling for his position. While the Heritage data address criminal activities only among undocumented immigrants who were *convicted*, Kevin took the liberty to associate these statistics with the undocumented immigrant community as a whole, which is how he was able to conclude his statement by saying that criminals constitute "the majority of people who are coming across the border." In other words, he bent the information to substantiate his own beliefs.

This strategy was successful, of course, despite the abundance of other data refuting his argument; scholars are in broad agreement that undocumented immigrants tend to commit less crime than natives (e.g., Gonzalez, Collingwood, & El-Khatib, 2017; Pérez-Péna, 2017). Perhaps Kevin was simply misinterpreting or misreading the data he discovered, or it might have simply been a case of seeing what he wanted to see and bringing that data into alignment with his existing ideas about immigration. Yet the zeal and conviction with which he presented those statistics raise the question of whether the result was less innocent, perhaps intentionally manipulated to serve as a more powerful argument for his case.

In her rejoinder, Latisha refrained from challenging Kevin's statistics, which might have been a result of the overwhelming amount of statistics he provided and/or her lack of knowing how to refute it. Perhaps she thought the statistics were sufficiently unworthy to be refuted. Instead, she chose to speak back to what was implied in Kevin's statistics—that criminality is inherent in, and a moral characteristic of, undocumented immigrants.

Latisha disputed Kevin's conclusions but not the premise on which they were based. Ironically, all Latisha needed to do in order to question Kevin's statistics was reference the evidence packet on her desk. However, like most other students during the deliberation, she chose not to use that resource.

Instead, Latisha inserted the issue of morality explicitly into the deliberation, suggesting that the criminality Kevin describes ought best to be attributed to the dire situation in which undocumented immigrants find themselves. In other words, she argued that they resort to such activity as a mode of survival rather than, as Kevin suggested, a key feature of their personal identity.

Responding, Kevin remained with the issue of morality but shifted its purview. For Latisha, morality related to character; for Kevin, morality equated with economic status. Poor people, he suggested, may be poor because they are immoral, and as the history he recounts suggests, people's poverty cannot be alleviated by allowing them into this country and providing them with social services. If we cannot raise them out of poverty, he concluded, the poor will continue to be immoral and criminals, thus putting a strain on the economy.

Once more, Kevin shared another set of statistics, this time found on ProCon.org, a website that promotes critical thinking and informed decision-making by presenting two sides of controversial public issues. Although ProCon.org (2017) presents the contrasting arguments side- by-side about immigration policy, Kevin, as he did in the earlier case, selected only those statistics that supported his current understanding about immigration and allowed him to make the case for restricting immigration policy.

Cherry-picking the data—rather than being open to other data that might cause one to think otherwise—are strategies associated with the phenomena of confirmation bias and motivated reasoning, found especially widely among highly partisan individuals. Indeed, as in the earlier exchange with Latisha, we see Kevin avoiding questions that challenge his assumptions. In the earlier example, it was questions regarding morality; here it is about the universality of his statement and what it might mean for American citizens who, too, are receiving more from the government than they financially contribute to it.

Rather than question his assumptions in response to Latisha, we see him doubling down, applying legality of status as a measure of whether someone is eligible for government assistance. Kevin was, of course, correct on this issue. However, being correct on the legality issue did not address the veracity of the data he presented. In fact, that very legality clause regarding eligibility for government assistance helped refute most of his argument.

Not only do undocumented immigrants pay more than $11.8 billion each year (as noted by Natalie), but they also pay sales tax on the goods and services they purchase (Anti-Defamation League, 2018). Further, according to Steven Gross, chief actuary for the Social Security Administration, undocumented immigrants "have contributed up to $300 billion, or nearly 10%, of the $2.7 trillion Social Security Trust Fund" (Davidson, 2013, para. 9). Yet undocumented immigrants are not eligible to receive its benefits, nor are they eligible for Medicaid, Medicare, and food stamps, as those require proof of legal status. In all, undocumented immigrants not only pay a higher tax rate than the richest Americans, they also benefit less as individuals from the system into which they pay.

Kevin, however, appeared not to be interested in evidence of this sort, which, like his own data, is easily accessible on the Internet, nor was he interested in evidence that did not speak to his convictions. He preferred instead to work with (and on) his own selective data, accepting it on faith, regardless of its veracity.

As the class deliberation continued, Natalie, in response to Kevin's last comments about the legality clause, proposed a solution:

Natalie (White female): Then why don't we solve the problem and make it legal? Why not make it easier for immigrants to come to this country so they're not doing it illegally?

Scott (White male): I think it's because resources are limited here. We don't just have an abundance of land or jobs or opportunities, and the people that are already born here should take precedence over those who are just coming in illegally.

Aaron (White male): It's not just jobs and stuff. It's land, food, water. We don't have an unlimited supply of land. We can't make more land. China has a population problem and they have laws to control it. We let our population get too big and we might see something like only one child per family or something like that.

Scott: That's the issue! If everyone comes in, then we're all going to be pretty much crammed in.

Adeeb (Middle Eastern male): There's a big difference. China is like 1.8 billion people compared to our 400 million.

Aaron: Well, if you add everyone . . .

Adeeb: And China is smaller than the USA also.

Aaron: Well, if you let every poor person in the world come into America or everyone who wanted to come into America, you're talking God knows how many people. . . . Then they bring their children and the population explodes.

Kevin: We already have so many poor people in the country right now that we just . . . [cross-talk]

Marini (African American female) [jumping in] What are you doing about the poor people who are here right now? . . . If the poor people were so important here, they'd be taken care of already. [cross talk] They aren't being taken care of.

Adam (White male): There's always going to be poor people. There is always going to be a bottom . . .

Natalie: So, you're not going to take care of them because there has to be somebody at the bottom?

Adam: But there has to be somebody at the bottom.

Latisha: Why can't you make that bottom better?

Adam: You can, but there's always going to be somebody at the bottom.

Hamid: If there's no bottom, then there's no economy.

Much like the first excerpt, though without the intensity of statistics that shut down other students' responses, this section illustrates how dubious assumptions and questionable, if not inaccurate, facts are mobilized to make claims. Underlying those claims is not necessarily an intent to mislead in order to "win" an argument, but an anxiety about an uncertain future and losing one's privileges (or one's economic status) by welcoming the unknown into one's domain. This anxiety triggers other positions related to defending U.S. national identity, for example, the stances of nativism, isolationism, and xenophobia. These postures also serve as defenses of capitalism, which appears here not only as an economic system, but also as an ideology.

The excerpt begins with Natalie proposing that if the legality issue, as Kevin suggested, is what results in undocumented immigrants drawing more from U.S. coffers than they contribute to them, why not legalize their status? To this question, Scott and Aaron responded by suggesting that the United States lacks sufficient land, food, water, or jobs to accommodate all those wanting to enter the country. Worried that "if everyone comes in, then we're all going to be pretty much crammed in," the students suggest that legalization may result in adoption of a one-child policy in the United States.

China, of course, no longer has a one-child policy (it ended in 2016), and it is larger in terms of square miles than the United States. While Aaron is correct in saying that "We don't have an unlimited supply of land. We can't make more land," such claims, including the possibility of a one-child policy here or the notion that this country does not have enough food or water to feed additional people, seem surprising given that a third of the food bought in the United States every day is thrown out (Chandler, 2016) and water shortages are problems of management as much as supply.

As for jobs, research suggests that rather than taking jobs from Americans, immigrants actually help create new jobs by buying U.S.-made products and starting their own businesses. In fact, studies have shown that "immigrants are twice as likely to start businesses as citizens born in the U.S., and companies owned by immigrants are more likely to hire employees than companies owned by native-born citizens." Also, "states with large numbers of immigrants report lower unemployment for everyone" (Anti-Defamation League, 2018, para. 5).

It appears, then, that the alarming "facts" they presented are not at the root of Scott and Aaron's statements, but rather the sense of anxiety they register about what might happen to them and their families if borders were opened to unrestricted immigration. It is likely an anxiety about losing power and control and sharing the land with others who are different from themselves that seems to be projected into this deliberation.

Adeeb's response that China was not a good comparison due to its much larger population does not seem to persuade or dissuade Aaron and Scott. When one is anxious about an imagined future that may put one's future in (imagined) peril, facts do not relieve those anxieties (Sharot, 2017; Weeks, 2015). Rather, they often further entrench anxieties that may exist. Despite Adeeb's challenges and corrections regarding the example of China, Aaron was not deterred, continuing his line of reasoning and hanging onto his convictions.

Kevin, the main speaker in the first excerpt, joined the foray by adding that we cannot worry about all of the poor people in the world who may want to come here because we have our own poor to worry about first. It is questionable, however, from Kevin's lack of response to Marini's statement ("If the poor people were so important here, they'd be taken care of already. They aren't being taken care of.") whether Kevin's insertion concerning this country's poor was meant to "rescue" Aaron and Scott from the exchange about China or add to it.

What Kevin's comment did stimulate was a shift to discussing not so much the poor as poverty and its place in the economic order of capitalism. What we find in the exchange is a fatalistic understanding: "There's always going to be poor people. There is always going to be a bottom"; and also, one of utility: "There has to be somebody at the bottom," supposedly in order to allow for a middle (which most of the students in class belong to) and a top (to which, it is assumed, they aspire).

This capitalist model of social and economic organization, in which some thrive at the expense of others and where the bottom must be larger to allow for a smaller top (the pyramid model), appeared to these students not as one economic model among several, but as the natural and inevitable order of things. Questions from Natalie ("So, you're not going to take care of them because there has to be somebody at the bottom?") or Latisha ("Why can't you make that bottom better?") remained unanswered. When one assumes the ideology of capitalism as destiny, such questions not only go unanswered, but also become unanswerable. After all, as suggested by Adeeb, "If there's no bottom, then there's no economy." What could be more anxiety-inducing than that?

DISCUSSION: USING, RESPONDING TO, AND MOVING BEYOND THE FACTS

In the previous sections of this chapter, we explored some specific aspects of the deliberation, directly corresponding to the transcripts provided. We use the space below to highlight broader issues underlying this deliberation and ones that go beyond it. Here we discuss the process in which facts are marshaled in order to make and refute claims, as well as how we might respond, as educators, to the notion that facts are often mobilized not simply as evidence in rational discourse, but also, and importantly, as support for the affective-laden processes of knowing and being in the world with others.

Using the original definition of deliberation, we expected students' engagement with the issue of immigration to produce a resolution to "a problem a 'we' faces," as Parker and Hess (2001, p. 282) put it. Little of that, however, took place. Instead, students considered the topic of immigration in ways that more closely resembled discussion, occasionally slipping into something slightly closer to debate, even though the students' verbal exchanges were not structured as a formal debate would have been. It may be that in an era of fake news, with the more rapid circulation of rumors, half-truths, and misinformation than of real information (Lazer et al., 2018), it is harder to move students from discussion to deliberation and consensus about resolution of a problem.

We also found that, although the class was almost evenly split between those supporting a more open, generous, and inclusive immigration policy and those who proposed further restrictions to immigration policy, as the excerpts illustrate, the anti-immigration side dominated the deliberation. Their "success" was not the result of their being the majority but rather because their discourse set the parameters, terms, and tone for the deliberation and was the one to which the proponents of more open immigration policy needed to respond. In this regard, and even though we saw the pro-immigration students clearly state their position, at times even challenging and baiting the proponents of restricted immigration policy, many of their contributions were in response to claims made by the latter. Rarely were the proponents of more open immigration able to set the agenda for the deliberation.

This finding highlights the idea that while most of the literature has focused on the truth or falsehood of particular facts entering public discourse or the ways in which motivated reasoning operates at the individual level, there is also a need to examine the role of misinformation in setting the agenda of civic deliberations, creating a ripple effect that allows the assertions of a single individual (whether a student or president) to shape the contours of the discussion. That such a discourse dynamic so dominated this deliberation is a broader problem to be addressed, both pedagogically as well as societally.

Although students pushed back on and challenged their peers' statements, little interrogation of the facts occurred, as if sourcing—an issue that appeared significant to students when examining data during the initial exercises of the study—seemed much less important in the free-wheeling context of the deliberation. This finding suggests that extant efforts to teach skills for critical examination of evidence are not necessarily lacking (though that may be an issue in some classrooms), but that these skills, even if they are demonstrated in written work, do not readily transfer into real-world deliberations, precisely the place social studies teachers hope these skills will be applied in discussing public policy issues.

As the excerpts shared within the chapter highlight, the role of truth or falsehood and its relation to fake news (both its propagation and consumption) and the impact of cognitive filters in producing confirmation bias and motivated reasoning were prevalent throughout the deliberation. Kevin provided the prime example of this phenomenon, although the conversations about the relative size of China versus the United States and potential scarcity of food and water also suggested the ways in which inaccurate information can circulate to advance particular arguments. Challenges to these assertions by other students did not shift the originators' opinions; they were not interested in facts, at least not ones that might challenge their "truth."

What should researchers and educators make of this situation? What might these data and analyses suggest about confronting fake news, confirmation bias, and motivated reasoning in classrooms? There seem to be no simple answers to these questions when deliberating about public issues. As in the civic square, the classroom space is one where students proclaim and assert preconceived notions about a topic rather than capitalizing on the opportunity for considering and possibly moving toward alternative understandings.

It is well to begin with the assumption that classroom deliberations are not necessarily the rational, reasoned, fact-based endeavors educators might hope for. Rather, classroom talk on controversial public policy issues is often more irrational, undisciplined, emotional, and visceral, not unlike real-world policy discussion.

Educators might pay more attention to these "other" forms of knowing and not-knowing that permeate classrooms. Students, like adults, may be motivated to learn, but they also avoid learning, affirm preconceived ideas, refuse knowledge, and defend themselves psychologically against evidence, news, or facts that trouble their assumptions and understandings of self, other, and the world more broadly.

We do not suggest that educators accept the presence of misinformation without challenge. Yet it is unclear what challenging misinformation might look like within the scope of a controversial issue discussion. The teacher in this study could have continually referred her students to the evidence packet; however, the facts included in that packet would not have necessarily addressed every piece of misinformation uttered in the discussion, nor is it reasonable to expect students not to bring outside knowledge into classroom discussions. The teacher could have also interrupted the discussion when she recognized incorrect facts; however, such corrections wade into dangerous territory. How can teachers be assured that they are not interjecting their own motivated reasoning and biased information into students' discussions?

Again, no simple answers exist to what is clearly a complex issue. What is clear is that educators need to acknowledge the presence (even prevalence) of misinformation as part of the human condition, which they must come to understand better and work with and through rather than merely ignore. To do the latter would be our own form of motivated reasoning, whereby educators ignore a reality simply because they do not like it or because it disturbs their existing or desired worldview and adherence to objective and rational modes of thinking.

NOTES

1. For more information on the various aspects of the study, see Crocco, Halvorsen, Jacobsen, and Segall (2017); Crocco, Halvorsen, Segall, and Jacobsen (2018); Crocco, Segall, Halvorsen, and Jacobsen (2018); and Jacobsen et al. (2018).

2. The question guiding the deliberation was "Which of these three positions do you think U.S. policymakers should focus on regarding immigration?" The three positions offered were: (1) Welcome anyone who wants to come into the country legally; (2) prevent undocumented immigrants from entering the country and deport all those already here; (3) allow only people with very specific job-related skills to enter.

REFERENCES

Alcorn, M. (2013). *Resistance to learning: Overcoming the desire not to know in classroom teaching*. New York, NY: Palgrave Macmillan.

Anti-Defamation League. (2018). Myths and facts about immigrants and immigration. Retrieved from www.adl.org/education/resources/fact-sheets/myths-and-facts-about-immigrants-and-immigration

Bowyer, B., & Kahne, J. (2017). Facing facts in an era of political polarization: Young people's learning and knowledge about economic inequality. *PS: Political Science & Politics, 50*, 1056–1061.

Breakstone, J., McGrew, S., Smith, M., Ortega, T., & Wineburg, S. (2018) Why we need a new approach to teaching digital literacy. *Phi Delta Kappan, 99*(6), 27–32.

Burmila, E. (2017, November 3). Why fake news works. *The Week*. Retrieved from theweek.com/articles/734306/why-fake-news-works

Chandler A. (2016, July 15). Why Americans lead the world in food waste. *The Atlantic*. Retrieved from www.theatlantic.com/business/archive/2016/07/american-food-waste/491513/

Crocco, M. S., Halvorsen, A.-L., Jacobsen, R. J., & Segall, A. (2017). Teaching with evidence. *Phi Delta Kappan, 98*(7), 67–71.

Crocco, M. S., Halvorsen, A.-L., Segall, A., & Jacobsen, R. J. (2018). Less arguing, more listening: Improving civility in classrooms. *Phi Delta Kappan, 99*(5), 67–71.

Crocco, M. S., Segall, A., Halvorsen, A.-L., & Jacobsen, R. J. (2018). Deliberating public policy issues with adolescents: Classroom dynamics and sociocultural considerations. *Democracy & Education, 26*(1). Retrieved from democracyeducationjournal.org/home/vol26/iss1/3/

Davidson, A. (2013, February 2). Do illegal immigrants actually hurt the U.S. economy? *The New York Times*. Retrieved from www.nytimes.com/2013/02/17/magazine/do-illegal-immigrants-actually-hurt-the-us-economy.html

Drobnic Holan, A. (2016, December 13). 2016 lie of the year: Fake news. *PolitiFact*. Retrieved from www.politifact.com/truth-o-meter/article/2016/dec/13/2016-lie-year-fake-news/

Felman, S. (1982). Psychoanalysis and education: Teaching terminable and interminable. *Yale French Studies, 63*, 21–44.

Flynn, D. J., Nyhan, B., & Reifler, J. (2016). The nature and origins of misperceptions: Understanding false and unsupported beliefs about politics. *Advances in Political Psychology, 38,* 127–150.

Garrett, H. J. (2017). *Learning to be in the world with others: Difficult knowledge and social studies education.* New York, NY: Peter Lang.

Gonzalez, B., Collingwood, L., & El-Khatib, S. O. (2017). The politics of refuge: Sanctuary cities, crime, and undocumented immigration. *Urban Affairs Review.* Retrieved from journals.sagepub.com/doi/abs/10.1177/1078087417704974?-journalCode=uarb

Jacobsen, R. J., Halvorsen, A.-L., Frasier, A., Schmitt, A., Crocco, M. S., & Segall, A. (2018). Thinking deeply, thinking emotionally: How high school students make sense of evidence. *Theory & Research in Social Education, 46,* 232–276.

Kahne, J., & Bowyer, B. (2017). Educating for democracy in a partisan age: Confronting the challenges of motivated reasoning and misinformation. *American Educational Research Journal, 54,* 3–34.

Kavanagh, J., & Rich, M. D. (2018). *Truth decay: An initial exploration of the diminishing role of facts and analysis in American public life.* Santa Monica, CA: RAND Corporation. Retrieved from www.rand.org/pubs/research_reports/RR2314.html

Kruglanski, A. (2017, September 15). Why do people believe fake news? *HuffPost.* Retrieved from www.huffingtonpost.com/entry/why-do-people-believe-fake-news_us_59bc73dde4b06b71800c396f

Lazer, D. M. J., Baum, M. A., Benkler, Y., Berinsky, A. J., Greenhill, K. M., Menczer, F., . . . Zittrain, J. L. (2018). The science of fake news. *Science, 35,* 1094–1096.

Levitan, D. J. (2016). *A field guide to lies: Critical thinking in the information age.* New York, NY: Dutton.

Lorch, M. (2017, August 18). Why people believe in conspiracy theories—and how to change their minds. *The Conversation.* Retrieved from theconversation.com/why-people-believe-in-conspiracy-theories-and-how-to-change-their-minds-82514

McGrew, S., Breakstone, J., Ortega, T., Smith, M., & Wineburg, S. (2018). Can students evaluate online sources? Learning from assessments of civic online reasoning. *Theory & Research in Social Education, 46,* 165–193.

The News Literacy Project. (2018). Checkology: Can your students tell the difference between fact and fiction? Retrieved from www.thenewsliteracyproject.org/services/checkology

Nyhan, B., & Reifler, J. (2010). When corrections fail: The persistence of political misperceptions. *Political Behavior, 32,* 303–330.

Oxford Dictionaries. (2016). Word of the year 2016 is . . . Retrieved from en.oxforddictionaries.com/word-of-the-year/word-of-the-year-2016

Parker, W. C., & Hess, D. (2001). Teaching with and for discussion. *Teaching and Teacher Education, 17,* 273–289.

Pérez-Péna, R. (2017, January 26). Contrary to Trump claims, immigrants are less likely to commit crimes. *The New York Times.* Retrieved from www.nytimes.com/2017/01/26/us/trump-illegal-immigrants-crime.html

Porter, T. M. (1996). *Trust in numbers: The pursuit of objectivity in science and public life.* Princeton, NJ: Princeton University Press.

ProCon.org. (2017, December 2). Should the government allow immigrants who are here illegally to become U.S. citizens? Retrieved from immigration.procon.org/

Sharot, T. (2017). *The influential mind: What the brain reveals about our power to change others*. New York, NY: Henry Holt.

Silverman, C., & Singer-Vine, J. (2016, December 6). Most Americans who see fake news believe it, new survey says. *BuzzFeed News*. Retrieved from www.buzzfeed.com/craigsilverman/fake-news-survey?utm_term=.snNeAx5xL#.tjDJN8Z8w

Turner, C,. & Lonsdorf, Kat. (2016, December 22). The classroom where fake news fails. *NPR* Ed [*All Things Considered*]. Retrieved from www.npr.org/sections/ed/2016/12/22/505432340/the-classroom-where-fake-news-fails

Von Spakovsky, H. A., & Strobl, G. (2017, March 13). What the media won't tell you about illegal immigration and criminal activity. *The Heritage Foundation*. Retrieved from www.heritage.org/immigration/commentary/what-the-media-wont-tell-you-about-illegal-immigration-and-criminal-activity

Weeks, B. E. (2015). Emotions, partisanship, and misperceptions: How anger and anxiety moderate the effect of partisan bias on susceptibility to political misinformation. *Journal of Communication*, 65, 699–719. doi: 10.1111/jcom.12164

Wineburg, S., & McGrew, S. (2017). *Lateral reading: Reading less and learning more when evaluating digital information* (Stanford History Education Group Working Paper No. 2017-A1). Retrieved from ssrn.com/abstract=3048994

Young, K. (2017). *Bunk: The rise of hoaxes, humbug, plagiarists, phonies, post-facts, and fake news*. Minneapolis, MN: Graywolf Press.

CHAPTER 6

Judging Credibility in Un-Credible Times

Three Educational Approaches for the Digital Age

Erica Hodgin and Joseph Kahne

In an 11th-grade social studies classroom in Chicago, Illinois, a teacher, Mr. Dudley, turns on the projector and shows his students a screencast of himself at a laptop. Students can see Mr. Dudley type several key terms into a search engine window, click around a few websites looking for more information, and check other sites to determine the credibility of the author and organization. They can also hear him think aloud by describing the thoughts and questions that come to mind.

After watching, students discuss what they saw Mr. Dudley doing and what strategies they could use in their own research project. The class is beginning a project in which they will identify an issue they care about, research the issue and a civic organization they believe is making a positive difference, and then interview a key civic actor in that organization. By making his process visible, Mr. Dudley surfaces the complexities of online research as well as the skills and stamina needed to navigate this new information landscape.

Investigating and researching civic and political issues on a local, state, national, and global level has always been a crucial element of civic and political life. However, in the past, information was identified, assessed, synthesized, and circulated for public consumption by institutional gatekeepers, such as scholars, journalists, the government, and interest group spokespeople based within formal organizations. Many organizations continue to play this role; however, the changing dynamics of the digital age have led to expanded opportunities for more participatory forms of investigation, as well as of publishing and circulating content.

Thus the degree to which information is now accessed through social networks and circulated without vetting has dramatically increased. This change has brought with it an increase in misinformation. Misinformation is not new, but its prevalence has grown with the rise of digital media tools and platforms.

For example, a Pew Research Center study conducted just after the 2016 presidential election found that 64% of adults believe fake news stories cause a great deal of confusion, and 23% said they had shared fabricated political stories themselves—sometimes by mistake and sometimes intentionally (Barthel, Mitchell, & Holcomb, 2016). Similarly, a 2017 Knight-Gallup survey found that 73% of Americans say the spread of inaccurate information on the Internet is a major problem with news coverage today; this percentage is higher than for any other potential type of news bias (Knight Foundation, 2018)

Not only has the information landscape changed, but so has the political landscape. The rising distrust in government and institutions, as well as intensifying partisanship, dramatically increased the challenges associated with "post-truth" politics in which the public relies less on objective facts when forming opinions and perspectives, especially when it comes to contentious or controversial issues (Anderson & Rainie, 2017).

In this context, one's views and opinions often cloud one's judgment, and individuals frequently favor ideas that align with their previously held beliefs independent of whether they are accurate. The Rand Corporation has described these dynamics as *truth decay*, which includes four key trends such as "an increasing disagreement about facts and analytical interpretations of facts and data; a blurring of the line between opinion and fact; an increase in the relative volume, and resulting influence, of opinion and personal experience over fact; and declining trust in formerly respected sources of factual information" (Kavanagh & Rich, 2018, para. 1).

In sum, changes in the media environment, such as the diminished role of gatekeepers and vastly expanded opportunities for circulation of both information and misinformation in the digital age, combined with increased partisanship and distrust in many formal institutions make exposure to and engagement with inaccurate information more common. These dynamics create a significant challenge for our democracy.

Of course, schools have long been charged with preparing youth for participation in our democracy. As John Dewey (1922) wrote in response to the rise of mass media technology, as well as political propaganda, after World War I: "The chief advantage of education is the assurance it gives of not being duped" (p. 329). Dewey posited that schools should prepare "young people to forge an active and empowered relationship to news and information" (Rogers, in press).

In order to understand the growth of misinformation and the challenges with assessing the credibility of information, one must focus on the underlying factors. In this chapter, we describe three particularly important factors:

- The challenge of assessing credibility with the spread of digital media tools and platforms
- The rising distrust in democracy and democratic institutions such as journalism
- The highly partisan nature of political life

Together, these factors create a context where information and misinformation abound, trust in the elite structures that define truth and credibility are waning, and our disrespect for those with differing perspectives means that we are less likely to question the veracity of news that aligns with our beliefs. In addition, we highlight in the chapter three important educational approaches that have the potential to promote young people's skills and capacities when it comes to research and investigation in the digital age.

INFORMATION IN THE DIGITAL AGE

The facile exchange of information and ideas in the digital age has clearly had a significant impact on youth. Ninety-two percent of U.S. teens (13–17 year olds) report going online daily, which includes 24% who say they go online "almost constantly" (Lenhart, 2015). Furthermore, political science and civic education scholars Cathy Cohen, Joseph Kahne, Benjamin Bowyer, Ellen Middaugh, and Jon Rogowski (2012) found that young people were as likely to receive news on civic and political issues from Twitter and Facebook posts by family and friends as they were from newspapers and magazines read both online and offline.

The opportunities to consume, circulate, and produce have fueled the rise of online *participatory politics*—interactive, peer-based acts through which individuals and groups seek to make their voices heard and exert influence on issues of public concern (Kahne, Middaugh, & Allen, 2014). Examples of participatory political acts range from blogging and circulating political news, to starting a new political group, to creating petitions, to mobilizing one's social network on behalf of a cause. Research shows that participatory politics has become a common form of participation, especially for youth (Cohen et al., 2012).

Similarly, communications studies scholar Paul Mihailidis (2014) found that young people use social media as the primary way that they communicate about politics, from voicing their opinions to sharing ideas and circulating content. Despite perceptions that digital media distracts youth from civic and political engagement, Mihailidis found that 48% of respondents agreed that social media has made them more aware of political issues, while over 85% disagreed with the idea that social media had lessened their awareness and commitments.

Although this heightened engagement clearly has benefits, youth and adults alike face an array of challenges in the information age including navigating the multitude of information online, judging the credibility and accuracy of sources and information, and considering the ethical decisions related to circulating information (or unwittingly circulating misinformation).

Recent studies show that adults and young people struggle a great deal to identify real from fake information. A research study including middle school, high school, and college students by the Stanford History Education Group showed that many youth struggle to judge the credibility of online information. For example, many youths could not tell the difference between a real news story and "sponsored content," or an advertisement (McGrew, Breakstone, Ortega, Smith, & Wineburg, 2018). Scholars have also found that youth often evaluate a website's credibility based on criteria such as the site's surface characteristics (Sundar, 2008) or whether the site was the first result provided by a search engine (Hargittai, Fullerton, Menchen-Trevino, & Thomas, 2010). These techniques for assessing credibility are typically not sufficient when evaluating political information.

In addition, since there are an array of options of news sources and exposure to news is often dependent on whom one follows on social media, these new forms of engagement foster greater exposure to like-minded people and information and lessen contact with divergent perspectives, creating an "echo chamber" of ideas (Prior, 2013; Sunstein, 2007). Moreover, some search engines and social media platforms have features that help tailor search results by feeding users information that aligns with their previous online activity, which helps reinforce limited exposure to diverse viewpoints and creates a "filter bubble" where readers view news media that aligns with their own perspectives (Pariser, 2011).

Although readers and viewers have always made choices about the media they consume, these dynamics may make the viral spread of politically motivated misinformation more prevalent and, at the same time, invisible to some extent (Rojecki & Meraz, 2016). As psychologists Stephen Lewandowsky, Ullrich Ecker, Colleen Seifert, Norbert Schwarz, and John Cook (2012) explain, both analytic and intuitive processing lead individuals to accept content that is consistent with their prior beliefs because it "feels right." This behavior can encourage individuals to accept misinformation as true and, when combined with participatory practices, to further spread falsehoods through social media.

Educational Implications of Information in the Digital Age

Clearly, the rise of digital media and the increasing prevalence of misinformation has significant implications for teaching and learning. In fact, a nationally representative group of youth were asked if they and their peers would benefit from learning how to tell whether information online was credible, and 84% said yes (Cohen et al., 2012). In a different study, a sample of 10–18-year-olds reported that following the news is important to them, and 50% said that it helped them feel prepared to make a difference in their communities (Robb, 2017).

Many experts agree that to be successful in this media-rich environment youth must develop *media literacy*—"the ability to access, analyze, evaluate, create, and act using all forms of communication" (National Association for Media Literacy Education, 2018, para. 1). In fact, social studies educator Jeremy Stoddard (2014) has argued that "the need for a media-savvy society is more important to our democracy than ever" as community members need to be able to understand the substance and influence of political information today (p. 2).

Educators are not only tasked with preparing youth to develop media literacy skills and strategies to investigate and research, but they must also respond to the misinformation that students find and share in the classroom. For example, a 2017 study found that 41% of teachers reported that students were more likely in this day and age to share unfounded claims from unreliable sources in classroom discussion (Rogers et al., 2017).

One Texas teacher shared how students had become more likely to "accept false and misleading 'news' stories as fact and refute or ignore verifiable news stories that are not in line with their existing political ideology," and thus they entered discussions with "more extreme and less tolerant viewpoints" (Rogers et al., 2017, p. 16). Therefore, educators play an increasingly critical role in helping young people not only navigate misinformation in their analysis of information but also engage in discussion and deliberation with others.

DISTRUST IN INSTITUTIONS AND THE MEDIA

The rise of digital media is not the only factor that has contributed to the challenge of assessing the credibility of information. Americans' declining trust in institutions in the last several decades is also a significant contributor. More specifically, polls show that there has been a pattern of declining trust in public schools, the medical system, organized religion, banks, the criminal justice system, and big corporations for the last four decades (Zuckerman, 2017).

For example, trust in the medical system has fallen from 80% in 1975 to 37% in 2015 (Zuckerman, 2017). In addition, The Pew Research Center (2014) found that less than 25% of people trust the federal government to do the right thing all or most of the time, which is down from 77% in 1964 when trust peaked. Furthermore, only three in ten Americans believe that their views are well represented in Washington (Agiesta, 2015).

Of particular importance here, Americans' trust and confidence in the mass media to "report the news fully, accurately, and fairly" has dropped to its lowest level in Gallup polling history, with only 32% saying they have a great deal or fair amount of trust in the media (Swift, 2016). Specifically, trust in newspapers has fallen from 51% in 1979 to 24% in 2015, and trust in television news has dropped from 46% in 1993 to 21% in 2015 (Zuckerman, 2017).

Despite declining trust, a 2017 survey showed that 84% of Americans still believe the news media plays a critical or very important role in democracy and in helping citizens stay informed (Knight Foundation, 2018). However, the same survey found that Americans do not think the news media is fulfilling their mission, and they struggle to identify an objective news source.

One important consequence of distrust in institutions and, in particular, news media is that it prompts a desire for alternative sources of information that better represent the experiences people have or the perspectives they believe. It has also led to what Kevin Kelly, cofounder of *Wired* magazine, described as "the new shape of truth." In a BBC article on "Lies, Propaganda, and Fake News," Kelly said: "Truth is no longer dictated by authorities, but is networked by peers. For every fact there is a counterfact and all these counterfacts and facts look identical online, which is confusing to most people" (Gray, 2017, para. 16).

Educational Implications of Distrust in Institutions and the Media

Educators play a critical role in helping young people productively reconcile their discontent with institutions, such as the news media, while at the same time, stressing the importance of high-quality journalism for democratic participation. A key ingredient of democracy is that citizens learn about issues by seeking out facts, evidence, and a range of perspectives in order to better inform their own opinions and decisions about how to respond and/or get involved. When facts and evidence are hard to identify and agree upon, it becomes challenging for democracy to function and for citizens to trust in democracy.

Educator Erik Palmer (2017) has argued that the more concerning aspect of fake news is not misinformation itself—as one can learn skills and strategies to identify it—but, rather, how to prevent total mistrust of the media. As he wrote, "For every person fooled by a fake story, there may be many more whose trust in the media in general is diminished. Discounting all news means discounting true news, too. And overwhelmingly, most news is true" (para. 4).

When the media and all news is discounted and deemed untrustworthy, one can choose to believe information that is based on one's ideological perspective without regard for credibility and accuracy. Given these dynamics, it is fundamentally important that educators support youth in developing a "healthy level of skepticism" so they are positioned to productively and critically evaluate media messages and information while at the same time understanding the role and value of the press in a democracy (Palmer, 2017, para. 6).

RISING PARTISANSHIP

The increasing partisan divide is also contributing to the challenge of misinformation. Studies show that conservatives and liberals differ in their beliefs about fundamental facts that relate to many of the most important issues in recent years, including the Iraq War (Kull, Ramsay, & Lewis, 2003), income inequality (Bartels, 2009), and climate change (McCright & Dunlap, 2011).

These partisan divides can influence the extent to which one judges the accuracy and credibility of information and claims. Social science research has found that when individuals encounter highly partisan issues, numerous biases influence their judgments of information and truth claims, as well as the degree to which individuals learn from exposure to and deliberation of new information.

In order to understand the biases that influence the way individuals process information, scholars underscore two fundamental motivations: *directional motivation* and *accuracy motivation* (Kunda, 1990; Taber & Lodge, 2006). Individuals can be guided by directional motivation or the desire to justify conclusions that align with prior beliefs. In this case, information that is consistent with one's prior preferences tends to be accepted uncritically and judged positively, whereas information that counters one's prior beliefs is scrutinized and often evaluated negatively (Ditto, Scepansky, Munro, Apanovitch, & Lockhart, 1998). On the other hand, when guided by accuracy motivation, individuals will exert more effort to carefully and deeply analyze information in order to understand issues (Kunda, 1990).

Directional motivation is particularly common when processing political information. For example, political scientists Milton Lodge and Charles Taber (2005) found that emotions often surface when engaging with sociopolitical concepts that, in turn, trigger "hot cognition," whereby positive and negative feelings bias subsequent information processing. This process leads individuals to seek out evidence that aligns with their preexisting views (*confirmation bias*), to attempt to dismiss perspectives that contradict their beliefs (*disconfirmation bias*), and to consider claims that align with their views as stronger and more accurate (*prior attitude effect*) (Kunda 1990; Taber & Lodge, 2006).

In short, directional motivation can constrain an individual's ability to learn from diverse viewpoints especially when it comes to politicized topics. In fact, political scientist David Redlawsk (2002) found that individuals who encountered new information that contradicted their prior perspective often become more convinced of their beliefs rather than learning from the new information.

Furthermore, in a study examining the ways in which prior beliefs shape judgment of the accuracy of political content circulated on social media, Kahne and Bowyer (2017) found that youth are guided by both directional motivation and accuracy motivation. However, they also found that prior beliefs had a greater impact than whether a given statement was accurate.

For example, youth tended to rate posts as "accurate" when the posts aligned with their prior views on the issue (irrespective of whether the post contained factual inaccuracies). In fact, on average, 67% of participants exposed to a post that aligned with their prior political views characterized the post as accurate, compared to 39% of those who saw a post that did not align with their prior political perspective (Kahne & Bowyer, 2017).

Educational Implications of Rising Partisanship

Partisanship and the dynamics related to directional motivation deserve careful attention from educators. In a media-rich environment in which political misinformation circulates widely and in which individuals can easily seek out like-minded news, the tendency to accept claims that align with one's beliefs will undermine the quality and ultimate productivity of democratic deliberation. Thus it is important for educators to help students recognize when they have strong beliefs and learn how to counteract the impact of directional motivation on their judgments of political content.

EDUCATIONAL APPROACHES FOR JUDGING THE CREDIBILITY OF ONLINE INFORMATION

Clearly, educators play an important role in supporting youth in developing ways of thinking, skills and strategies, and habits needed to navigate this media-rich and highly partisan civic and political landscape. Unfortunately, media literacy instruction that supports youth in judging the credibility of civic and political information found online is lacking. In a 2013 study, 33% of high school age youth did not report a single class session that focused on how to tell if information found online was trustworthy, and only 16% reported having more than a few class sessions focused on this topic (Kahne, Hodgin, & Eidman-Aadahl, 2016).

Yet research demonstrates that civic media literacy education can be significantly beneficial (Kahne & Bowyer, 2017). Specifically, young people who received civic media literacy learning opportunities were 26% more likely to judge an accurate political post on social media as "accurate" than they were to judge an inaccurate post as "accurate," even when both posts aligned with their perspective on an issue. In contrast, youth with no civic media literacy learning were just as likely to judge inaccurate posts as accurate as they were posts that used factual evidence. Likewise, when youth whose teachers taught about judging the credibility of content were shown a post and asked if they would retweet it, they were less likely to say they would (if the post was inaccurate) than were youth whose teachers had not taught about making credibility judgments.

Communication studies scholars Hans Martens and Renee Hobbs (2015) similarly found that students enrolled in a school-based media literacy program demonstrated better advertisement analysis skills and media knowledge than students from the same school who did not participate in the program. Therefore, it is critical for schools and community-based educational institutions to integrate civic media literacy learning opportunities that attend to these challenges in order to prepare students to navigate the complex information and political landscape.

At the same time, providing all youth with equitable access to high-quality civic media literacy education must be a central concern of any effort. While these opportunities are relevant for all school contexts, they are particularly important to address in underresourced schools. In fact, communications studies scholar Eszter Hargittai (2010) found that Internet skill level increases correspondingly with students' socioeconomic status. Moreover, on average, White students, middle-class students, and students in higher-track classes experience more classroom-based, after-school, and informal civic learning opportunities (Kahne & Middaugh, 2008).

Thus in order to attend to the inequitable provision of high-quality digital learning opportunities, educational institutions will need to put in place a range of supports including improved infrastructure, professional development, curricular resources, and administrative support and leadership.

Drawing on studies we have conducted, we describe three approaches to civic media literacy education that our findings suggest are key for attending to the relationship between digital media and misinformation:

1. Educators can support youth in developing metacognition related to judging the accuracy and credibility of online information.
2. Educators can provide youth with more nuanced skills and strategies for assessing the accuracy of truth claims.
3. Educators can provide young people with ongoing opportunities to reflect and practice the skills and strategies they have learned in order to instill habits that will transfer across various settings.

In fact, these three approaches are not unlike how educators often structure pedagogical approaches toward other curricular endeavors. Specifically, teachers support students in building a deep awareness of the issue at hand, in developing a range of skills and strategies to address the challenge, and in practicing so that they can continue to apply what they have learned in the future. Taken together, the three approaches we describe below have the potential to support young people in identifying bias and misinformation, critically assessing factual claims, and forming their own opinions and arguments about pressing issues affecting their communities and society.

Building Metacognition

In order to assess the credibility and accuracy of information, young people may benefit from developing an awareness of the role their individual thinking plays in understanding and evaluating information and in reflecting on their own personal biases in relationship to that analysis. *Metacognition*—the awareness of one's learning processes—often takes the form of an internal dialogue where students are thinking about their own thinking (Biggs, 1987; Bransford, Brown, & Cocking, 2000).

Educators can help make metacognitive processes visible to students in order to surface the kinds of sense-making, self-assessment, and reflection that can enable students to productively analyze online information and recognize what they are learning, what strategies worked, and what needs improving. For example, in the opening example of this chapter, Mr. Dudley made his own thinking visible to students as he shared a recording of himself thinking aloud about the process of searching and evaluating information on various websites. By watching this demonstration, students were given a window into the kind of internal dialogue that can be integrated into their own thinking and analysis when conducting research.

In addition, educators can help students acknowledge their own opinions and how those may influence their evaluation of a claim. By understanding how their prior beliefs may elicit positive or negative feelings that bias their processing of information, students can work to ensure these triggered reactions do not eclipse their efforts to assess the accuracy and credibility of an argument. For example, teachers can support students in developing what political psychologists Howard Lavine, Christopher Johnston, and Marco Steenbergen (2012) called "critical loyalty." Those with critical loyalty still hold strong values and beliefs, but they adopt a critical stance when evaluating an argument—even when it aligns with their beliefs.

In the classroom, educators can highlight metacognitive processes that can strengthen students' ability to evaluate the accuracy and credibility of varied political claims while stressing the need to carefully assess one's biases. For example, one high school English teacher named Ms. Moa worked with 12th-grade students in an urban school district in Oakland, California, to write a series of blog posts reflecting on their thinking and learning as they researched a pressing social issue for a capstone project.

Students wrote numerous posts over the course of the project. For example, after doing some initial research, students paused and chronicled what they found, what sources were reliable and why, what challenges they faced, and what they could do next to deepen their research. Students read their classmates' posts and uploaded comments in order to offer thoughts and advice. This process also enabled students to learn about the metacognition of their peers.

Finally, at the end of the project, Ms. Moa asked students to read back over their blog posts and reflect on how their thinking evolved as well as what they had learned. We saw evidence that this kind of reflective writing stressed the importance of attending to accuracy and credibility, and it also illustrated how students' opinions and perspectives about the issue itself had shifted over time.

Developing Nuanced Skills and Strategies

In addition, educators can provide students with nuanced skills and strategies for assessing the accuracy of truth claims that move beyond hard and fast rules or rote checklists. Such rules and lists misrepresent how complex online information has become and, therefore, may make students more susceptible to believing misinformation (McGrew et al., 2018). For example, superficial characteristics such as the polished "look" of a website or whether the domain is ".com" or ".org" are not reliable features by which to judge the credibility of a website. Instead, educators can help students understand the complexity that exists and explicitly teach a range of skills and strategies youth can utilize to navigate the online information landscape.

McGrew et al. (2018) of the Stanford History Education Group call these kind of strategies *civic online reasoning*—"the ability to effectively search for, evaluate, and verify social and political information online" (p. 2)—which includes the ability to identify who is behind a piece of information, evaluate the evidence, and investigate additional sources. In a classroom, educators might highlight strategies for choosing between the various results of a search, checking the reliability and credibility of sources, and finding background information on groups making varied claims by looking on a range of websites.

For instance, a 9th-grade English teacher named Ms. Richards in Oakland, California, helped her students learn to judge the credibility of different online sources in preparation for a research project on a contemporary civil rights issue. While reading articles about New York's controversial "Stop and Frisk" policy, Ms. Richards asked students to use a "Trust-O-Meter" that included a series of critical inquiry questions that guided students in assessing whether a source was trustworthy, thereby highlighting factors that made a source questionable or untrustworthy (Middaugh & Evans, 2016). By weighing the strengths and weaknesses of a source, Ms. Richards found that students were better able to determine the credibility of the online sources as well as reflect on the complexity of such a task.

A number of organizations have created curricular resources that help students in developing skills and strategies for judging the credibility of online information. The News Literacy Project, for example, developed an online platform called Checkology where students participate in a series of interactive lessons hosted by real-world professionals and focus on topics such as critiquing news judgments, dissecting viral rumors, interpreting and applying the First Amendment, investigating the impact of personalization algorithms, and learning about confirmation bias.[1]

Offering Ongoing Opportunities for Practice

Finally, our studies suggest that it is important for students to be given multiple opportunities to practice judging the credibility of online information in a range of ways. Ongoing and varied practice can help students integrate these ways of thinking and these skills and strategies into their habits, which can then be applied across settings and contexts. In a study involving high school students, Middaugh (2017) found that in order for youth to make fluent and flexible use of the media literacy skills and strategies they learned, students needed lots of practice.

While finding time and space for additional content is certainly a challenge, many teachers we collaborated with found success by integrating digital civic media learning opportunities throughout the core curriculum in ways that deepened and extended students' learning (Kahne, Evans, Hodgin, & Choi, 2018). In addition, the quality of such opportunities for practice is key to consider as well. Mihailidis (2009) found that media literacy education approaches that focus solely on skill attainment result in less interest and engagement by students. Undoubtedly, offering ongoing learning opportunities that are relevant, authentic, and related to students' interests is critical.

Ms. Blake, a high school humanities teacher outside Dallas, Texas, integrated regular opportunities for her students to practice judging the credibility of online information via a weekly activity at the start of class. Students responded to a current event via Twitter using a common hashtag and briefly sharing their perspective on the issue. Ms. Blake drew on content developed by KQED—a public media station in northern California—through a program called "Do Now" in which students across the country responded to and engaged in an online discussion centered around a weekly question about a timely and relevant current event. In their response, Ms. Blake asked students to include at least one link to a credible source they found that backed up their opinion, which meant students had to conduct some initial research, determine the credibility and reliability of a variety of sources, and weigh what they had learned against their ideas in order to succinctly state their opinion.

This classroom routine gave students the opportunity to refine their skills and strategies analyzing sources, assessing accuracy and bias, and reflecting on multiple perspectives on a range of civic and political issues. It appears that this type of ongoing opportunity enabled students to become more effective and confident in their research skills, as well as allowing them to see how such techniques can be applied to a range of topics and projects.

IMPLICATIONS

The changes in the online information landscape, the growing distrust in democratic institutions, and the highly partisan nature of political life have all contributed to the growth of misinformation and made assessing the credibility of information challenging for youth and adults alike. Experts agree that there are troubling impacts on our democracy as a result of misinformation. However, there is no agreement on whether false and misleading information online will improve or get worse as a result of technological changes designed to reduce misinformation (Anderson & Rainie, 2017).

Despite this uncertainty, there are multiple ways to respond productively to the challenges we face, and education clearly has a significant role to play. While we have much to learn, studies have found that high-quality civic media literacy education can be beneficial (Kahne & Bowyer, 2017; Martens & Hobbs, 2015). In addition, research shows that large numbers of students are not receiving the civic education necessary to support informed and active participation in civic and political life (Gould, Jamieson, Levine, McConnell, & Smith, 2011). At the same time, in order for the kinds of civic media literacy education described in this chapter to be integrated across the curriculum for all students, teachers must be given support, resources, and opportunities to deepen their own metacognition and expand their skills and strategies.

For example, a survey of U.S. teachers involved in literacy education found that lack of time was the most significant obstacle to the implementation of digital literacy courses, followed by the lack of access to technology, lack of training to enable them to teach the material, lack of technical support, and lack of incentives (Hutchinson & Reinking, 2011). Another study noted the lack of administrative support for the integration of digital literacy into the school curricula (Drew, 2012/2013).

Furthermore, teacher education programs have an ever-increasing role to play in supporting and guiding teachers in building the knowledge and skills needed to bridge subject area content, pedagogy, and the affordances of digital tools across content areas (Neiss, 2011). For instance, social studies scholar Wayne Journell (2009) has described the need for digital literacy integration into social studies methods courses so that preservice teachers can see practical applications to classroom practice. In short, it will take a commitment and an investment from teacher education, educational policymakers, funders, districts, and schools in order to provide teachers with the support, time, space, and resources needed to make these efforts a priority.

Educational institutions and educators must provide equitable and high-quality civic media literacy learning opportunities so that all youth will be able to develop metacognition, skills and strategies, as well as habits that can enable them to identify bias and misinformation, critically assess factual claims, and form their own opinions and arguments about pressing issues affecting their communities and society. In turn, this type of instruction can support youth in becoming more effective and thoughtful civic actors in the digital age and even possibly help repair distrust and disengagement in democratic life.

NOTE

1. For other organizations focused on media and news literacy and concerned with helping students determine the credibility of online resources, see: The Center for Media Literacy, Center for News Literacy, Common Sense Education, Facing History and Ourselves, KQED Education, Media Education Lab, NewseumEd, and Teaching Tolerance's Digital and Civic Literacy resources. These organizations have collections of resources on their websites that are available for educators to access and use.

REFERENCES

Agiesta, J. (2015, July 27). What's behind the Trump bump? A disgruntled GOP electorate. *CNN Politics*. Retrieved from www.cnn.com/2015/07/27/politics/donald-trump-cnn-orc-poll-2016/index.html

Anderson, J., & Rainie, L. (2017). The future of trust and misinformation online. *Pew Research Center*. Retrieved from www.pewinternet.org/2017/10/19/the-future-of-truth-and-misinformation-online

Barthel, M., Mitchell, A., & Holcomb, J. (2016, December). Many Americans believe fake news is sowing confusion. *Pew Research Center*. Retrieved from www.journalism.org/2016/12/15/many-americans-believe-fake-news-is-sowing-confusion/

Bartels, L. M. (2009). *Unequal democracy: The political economy of the new Gilded Age*. Princeton, NJ: Princeton University Press.

Biggs, J. B. (1987). *Student approaches to learning and studying*. Hawthorn, Victoria: Australian Council for Educational Research.

Bransford, J. D., Brown, A. L., & Cocking, R. R. (Eds.). (2000). *How people learn: Brain, mind, experience, and school*. Washington, DC: National Academy Press.

Cohen, C., Kahne, J., Bowyer, B., Middaugh, E., & Rogowski, J. (2012). *Participatory politics: New media and youth political action* [YPPSP Research Report]. Oakland, CA: Youth and Participatory Politics Research Network. Retrieved from ypp.dmlcentral.net/publications/107

Dewey, J. (1922). Education as politics. In *The middle works of John Dewey, Volume 13, 1899–1924: 1921–1922, Essays on philosophy, education, and the Orient* (pp. 329–336). Carbondale, IL: Southern Illinois University Press.

Ditto, P. H., Scepansky, J. A., Munro, G. D., Apanovitch, A. M., & Lockhart, L. K. (1998). Motivated sensitivity to preference-inconsistent information. *Journal of Personality and Social Psychology*, *75*, 53–69.

Drew, S. V. (2012/2013). Open up the ceiling on Common Core State Standards: Preparing students for 21st-century literacy—now. *Journal of Adolescent & Adult Literacy*, *56*, 321–330.

Gould, J., Jamieson, K. H., Levine, P., McConnell, T., & Smith, D. B. (Eds.). (2011). *Guardian of democracy: The civic mission of schools*. Philadelphia, PA: Lenore Annenberg Institute for Civics of the Annenberg Public Policy Center and the Civic Mission of Schools.

Gray, R. (2017, March 1). Lies, propaganda and fake news: A challenge for our age. *BBC: Future Now.* Retrieved from www.bbc.com/future/story/20170301-lies-propaganda-and-fake-news-a-grand-challenge-of-our-age

Hargittai, E. (2010). Digital na(t)ives? Variation in Internet skills and uses among members of the "Net Generation." *Sociological Inquiry*, *80*, 92–113.

Hargittai, E., Fullerton, L., Menchen-Trevino, E., & Thomas, K. Y. (2010). Trust online: Young adults' evaluation of Web content. *International Journal of Communication*, *4*, 468–494.

Hutchinson, A., & Reinking, D. (2011). Teachers' perceptions of integrating information and communication technologies into literacy instruction: A national survey in the United States. *Reading Research Quarterly*, *46*, 312–333.

Journell, W. (2009). Maximizing the potential of computer-based technology in secondary social studies education. *Social Studies Research and Practice, 4*, 55–70.

Kahne, J., & Bowyer, B. (2017). Educating for democracy in a partisan age: Confronting the challenges of motivated reasoning and misinformation. *American Educational Research Journal*, *54*, 3–34.

Kahne, J., Evans, C., Hodgin, E., & Choi, Y. W. (2018). Equitable education for democracy in the digital age: A district-wide approach. In W. G. Tierney, Z. B. Corwin, & A. Ochsner (Eds.), *Diversifying digital learning: Online literacy and educational opportunity* (pp. 25–44). Baltimore, MD: John Hopkins University Press.

Kahne, J., Hodgin, E., & Eidman-Aadahl, E. (2016). Redesigning civic education for the digital age: Participatory politics and the pursuit of democratic engagement. *Theory & Research in Social Education, 44*, 1–35.

Kahne, J., & Middaugh, E. (2008, February). *Democracy for some: The civic opportunity gap in high school* [CIRCLE Working Paper 59]. Retrieved from www.civicyouth.org/PopUps/WorkingPapers/WP59Kahne.pdf

Kahne, J., Middaugh, E., & Allen, D. (2014). *Youth, new media, and the rise of participatory politics* [YPP Research Network Working Papers No. 1]. Oakland, CA: Youth and Participatory Politics Research Network. Retrieved from ypp.dmlcentral.net/sites/default/files/publications/YPP_WorkinPapers_Paper01_8.24.17.pdf

Kavanagh, J., & Rich, M. D. (2018). *Truth decay: An initial exploration of the diminishing role of facts and analysis in American public life*. Santa Monica, CA: RAND Corporation, Retrieved from www.rand.org/pubs/research_reports/RR2314.html

Knight Foundation (2018). *American views: Trust, media, and democracy*. Miami, FL: Knight Foundation. Retrieved from knightfoundation.org/reports/american-views-trust-media-and-democracy

Kull, S., Ramsay, C., & Lewis, E. (2003). Misperceptions, the media, and the Iraq war. *Political Science Quarterly*, *118*, 569–598.

Kunda, Z. (1990). The case for motivated reasoning. *Psychological Bulletin*, *108*, 480–498.

Lavine, H. G., Johnston, C. D., & Steenbergen, M. R. (2012). *The ambivalent partisan: How critical loyalty promotes democracy*. Oxford, United Kingdom: Oxford University Press.

Lenhart, A. (2015). Teens, social media & technology overview 2015. *Pew Research Center*. Retrieved from www.pewinternet.org/2015/04/09/teens-social-media-technology-2015/

Lewandowsky, S., Ecker, U. K. H., Seifert, C. M., Schwarz, N., & Cook, J. (2012). Misinformation and its correction: Continued influence and successful debiasing. *Psychological Science in the Public Interest*, *13*, 106–131.

Lodge, M., & Taber, C. (2005). Implicit affect for political candidates, parties, and issues: An experimental test of the hot cognition hypothesis. *Political Psychology, 26*, 455–482.

Martens, H., & Hobbs, R. (2015). How media literacy supports civic engagement in the digital age. *Journal of Communication*, *23*, 120–137.

McCright, A. M., & Dunlap, R. E. (2011). The politicization of climate change and polarization in the American public's views of global warming, 2001–2010. *The Sociological Quarterly*, *52*, 155–194.

McGrew, S., Breakstone, J., Ortega, T., Smith, M., & Wineburg, S. (2018). Can students evaluate online sources? Learning from assessments of civic online reasoning. *Theory & Research in Social Education, 46*, 165–193.

Middaugh, E. (2017, November). *When media literacy meets issue advocacy: Adolescents' use of media literacy strategies in civic inquiry.* Paper presented at the annual meeting of the College and University Faculty Assembly of the National Council for the Social Studies, San Francisco, CA.

Middaugh, E., & Evans, C. (2016). *From theory to practice: Fostering digital civic literacy in urban classrooms*. Manuscript in preparation.

Mihailidis, P. (2009). Beyond cynicism: Media education and civic learning outcomes in the university. *International Journal of Learning and Media, 1*(3), 1–13.

Mihailidis, P. (2014). *Media literacy and the emerging citizen: Youth, engagement and participation in digital culture*. New York, NY: Peter Lang.

National Association for Media Literacy Education (NAMLE). (2018, February 1). Media literacy defined. Retrieved from namle.net/publications/media-literacy-definitions/

Neiss, M. (2011). Investigating TPACK: Knowledge growth in teaching with technology. *Journal of Educational Computing Research*, *44*, 299–317.

Palmer, E. (2017). The real problem with fake news. *Educational Leadership, 75*(3). Retrieved from www.ascd.org/publications/educational-leadership/nov17/vol75/num03/The-Real-Problem-with-Fake-News.aspx

Pariser, E. (2011, March). *Beware online "filter bubbles"* [Video file]. Retrieved from www.ted.com/talks/eli_pariser_beware_online_filter_bubbles

Pew Research Center. (2014). Public trust in government: 1958–2014. Retrieved from www.people-press.org/2014/11/13/public-trust-in-government/

Prior, M. (2013). Media and political polarization. *Annual Review of Political Science, 16*, 101–127.

Redlawsk, D. P. (2002). Hot cognition or cool consideration? Testing the effects of motivated reasoning on political decision making. *Journal of Politics, 64*, 1021–1044.

Robb, M. B. (2017). *News and America's kids: How young people perceive and are impacted by the news.* San Francisco, CA: Common Sense. Retrieved from www.commonsensemedia.org/sites/default/files/uploads/research/2017_commonsense_newsandamericaskids.pdf

Rogers, J. (in press). Education for 'not being duped' in an era of fake news: Insights from John Dewey and Paulo Freire. In C. Torres (Ed.), *The Wiley handbook of Paulo Freire.*

Rogers, J., Franke, M., Yun, J.-E. E., Ishimoto, M., Diera, C., Geller, R. C., . . . Brenes, T. (2017). *Teaching and learning in the age of Trump: Increasing stress and hostility in America's high schools.* Los Angeles: University of California–Los Angeles, Institute for Democracy, Education, and Access. Retrieved from idea.gseis.ucla.edu/publications/teaching-and-learning-in-age-of-trump

Rojecki, A., & Meraz, S. (2016). Rumors and factitious informational blends: The role of the Web in speculative politics. *New Media & Society, 18*, 25–43.

Stoddard, J. (2014). The need for media education in democratic education. *Democracy & Education, 22*(1), 1–9.

Sundar, S. S. (2008). The MAIN model: A heuristic approach to understanding technology effects on credibility. In M. J. Metzger & A. J. Flanagin (Eds.), *Digital media, youth, and credibility* (pp. 73–100). Cambridge, MA: MIT Press.

Sunstein, C. R. (2007). *Republic.com 2.0.* Princeton, NJ: Princeton University Press.

Swift, A. (2016). Americans' trust in mass media sinks to new low. *Gallup News.* Retrieved from news.gallup.com/poll/195542/americans-trust-mass-media-sinks-new-low.aspx

Taber, C. S., & Lodge, M. (2006). Motivated skepticism in the evaluation of political beliefs. *American Journal of Political Science, 50*, 755–769.

Zuckerman, E. (2017). *Mistrust, efficacy and the new civics: Understanding the deep roots of the crisis of faith in journalism.* Knight Commission Workshop on Trust, Media and American Democracy. Retrieved from assets.aspeninstitute.org/content/uploads/2017/07/zuckerman.whitepaper.FINAL_.pdf

CHAPTER 7

Political Memes and the Limits of Media Literacy

Wayne Journell and Christopher H. Clark

Over the past decade, memes have become ubiquitous in social media discourse. These days, it is almost impossible to scroll through Facebook, Twitter, or any other social media outlet and not encounter a meme. These often simple visuals are easily created, and a popular meme can quickly spread across the social media landscape, potentially reaching and influencing millions of people. As communications scholar Limor Shifman (2014) has noted, "Ostensibly, [memes] are trivial pieces of pop culture; yet a deeper look reveals that they play an integral part in some of the defining events of the twenty-first century" (p. 6).

Memes come in multiple forms, but their purpose is to send a message and evoke a response. Although that message is often humorous (e.g., memes that poke fun at rival sports teams or parody plotlines of popular television shows), memes are increasingly being used to provide commentary about social and political issues of the day. These types of memes often serve to demonize opposing viewpoints and thus have helped contribute to the political polarization of American society.

Political memes pose unique challenges for teaching about media literacy. Since memes' authorship and intent are difficult to trace, they cannot be analyzed using the same techniques as traditional forms of media. They cannot be categorically dismissed, either. Memes have become part of the cultural lexicon, and students are sure to encounter political memes on a regular basis, likely more often than they read traditional news sources. Therefore, a critical understanding of political memes is essential for civic education in the 21st century.

In the remainder of this chapter, we provide historical, academic, and cultural definitions of "meme" and then discuss how memes can be used for political purposes. Using tenets of political psychology, we then discuss why political memes are effective as a form of political persuasion. We conclude by arguing that current approaches to media literacy education are limited when it comes to understanding political memes, and we offer suggestions for how teachers might effectively broach political memes in their classes.

WHAT ARE MEMES?

The term *meme* was coined by Richard Dawkins, a biologist, in his 1976 book, *The Selfish Gene*. For Dawkins, memes represented cultural "genes" that could be transmitted from person to person. Examples of cultural memes offered by Dawkins ranged from the mundane (e.g., musical melodies, popular catchphrases) to the existential (e.g., belief in God). Dawkins argued that memes follow evolutionary theory, meaning that they stay ubiquitous as long as they remain relevant to the sociocultural context in which they were created; if they cease to be relevant, they become extinct (Shifman, 2014).

An illustrative example of this type of meme can be found in the famous "Kilroy was here" drawings that appeared in the United States and in places occupied by American troops during World War II. The origin of the drawing, which contained the aforementioned phrase along with a simple drawing of a man with a large nose peering over a wall, has been debated, but most attribute it to a Massachusetts wharf inspector, James Kilroy, who used the phrase to indicate that a ship had passed inspection.

After the ships had been inspected, they were sent to various places in the European theatre. As American soldiers began seeing the phrase on their ships, they, for unknown reasons, began replicating it, adding in the famous face, in public places across Europe. When the soldiers came home, they shared the meme with friends and family, and it began appearing in public places across the United States. Once the war ended, however, the fascination with Kilroy waned. Public depictions of the meme appeared less frequently, and within a couple of decades it had almost completely vanished from American culture (Shifman, 2014; Williams, 1999).

Although much has been written about Dawkins's use of the term, a detailed discussion of the merits of Dawkins's argument is beyond the scope of this chapter. Our interest lies in the way Internet users have appropriated the term. A search of the term *Internet meme* on Google Trends shows that although the term existed in 2004, which is as far back as Google Trends tracks search queries, it seems to have become a relevant part of Internet culture only in the past decade. In other words, Internet memes are a relatively new social phenomenon.

This brief history of Internet memes, coupled with the continual evolution of social media platforms, has made defining contemporary use of the term *meme* challenging. In an academic sense, memes are "groups of digital items sharing common characteristics of content, form, and/or stance, which were created with awareness of each other, and were circulated, imitated, and/or transformed via the Internet by many users" (Shifman, 2014, p. 41). A viral video, then, would not meet the academic definition of a meme; however, if that viral video spawned multiple parodies that were applied to a range of contexts, then those parodies would be considered memes.

An illustrative example of this academic definition can be seen in the popular Kermit Sipping Tea memes that regularly circulate on social media. The meme is a picture of Kermit the Frog drinking a glass of iced tea, and Internet users typically include a snarky phrase that highlights a perceived hypocrisy, followed by the words, "But that's none of my business." Figure 7.1 provides two examples of the Kermit meme.

A Google Image search of "Kermit Tea Meme" generates hundreds of memes that have the same basic structure. The messages associated with the memes, however, range from the petty (e.g., making fun of gym goers taking selfies) to the obscene. As Figure 7.1 illustrates, a considerable number also could be construed as political in nature. Again, these memes all meet the academic definition of the term since they share common characteristics and were obviously created with an awareness of the general premise behind the Kermit Sipping Tea meme.

This academic definition of meme, however, is not necessarily the same one used by Internet users. Internet users would correctly identify the images in Figure 7.1 as memes, but most would also apply the same term to any number of text- and/or image-based posts that are shared widely on social media. While we appreciate the reasons for the specificity given in the academic definition provided above, it is likely too narrow from a pedagogical standpoint, given that, for most students, memes serve as a genre of online communication that is indicative of discourse in the digital age (Wiggins & Bowers, 2015).

Perhaps, then, a more appropriate definition for the purposes of this chapter is the one posited by new literacies scholars Michelle Knobel and Colin Lankshear (2007) who describe memes as "a particular idea presented as a written text, image, language 'move,' or some other unit of cultural stuff'" (p. 202). This definition lacks the replication element of the academic definition that harkens back to Dawkins's original use of the term; however, political memes, in particular, are often created "in the moment" and may not necessarily be meant to fit within a preexisting format. Therefore, we will use this more informal definition to frame the rest of the chapter.

HOW MEMES ARE USED FOR POLITICAL PURPOSES

According to Shifman (2014), "political memes are about making a point—participating in a normative debate about how the world should look and the best way to get there" (p. 120). Although meme creation cannot be quantified in the same way as traditional measures of political participation

Figure 7.1. Two Examples of the Kermit Sipping Tea Meme

(e.g., voting), making one's position known and sharing that position online is a political act, one that has the potential to influence an untold number of people. It is also a political act in which young people participate, one of the subtle ways that young people are combating the stereotype that American youth are politically disengaged (Journell, 2017).

There is considerable evidence to suggest that political memes are influential in helping shape or reinforce people's political views and their opinions on political figures.[1] Several scholars, for example, credit memes as helping sway people's opinions about the Occupy Wall Street movement in 2011 (Huntington, 2016; Milner, 2013). Journalist Ari Melber (2012) went so far as to dub the 2012 presidential election "the first meme election" and argued that memes allow everyday Americans, instead of traditional media outlets, the opportunity to define political narratives.

Political memes are often humorous in nature, but underneath the humor is a serious message. For example, following the election of Barack Obama, conservatives responded with a host of "Thanks, Obama" memes that sarcastically thanked the president for things they perceived as negative (e.g., growing the national debt). After a couple of years, the meme remained, but the message had shifted. Liberals, exasperated at the blame being placed on Obama, appropriated the "Thanks, Obama" tagline and created memes that "thanked" the president for everyday inconveniences, such as burning toast (Schwartz, 2015).

For the politicians who become the face of memes, the outcome is usually damaging.[2] During the 2012 election, for example, Mitt Romney's debate claim that he had used "binders full of women" to ensure that he hired equitable numbers of women during his tenure as governor of Massachusetts turned into a meme that hounded him the remainder of the campaign (Tay, 2015). Similarly, unflattering pictures of Hillary Clinton laughing or appearing to be wildly screaming became fodder for a host of right-wing memes that were shared widely on social media during the 2016 election.

Given that many political issues are often intertwined with issues of race, gender, sexuality, and religion (Journell, 2011, 2016), political memes can often be racist, sexist, xenophobic, or bigoted in nature (Yoon, 2016).[3] Oftentimes, this bigotry is shrouded in humor, such as in the case of a Kermit Sipping Tea meme about #BlackLivesMatter protests that turned violent in which the meme author questioned why the local welfare office was not looted. Internet users who share such memes, either because they agree with the political stance being presented or find them humorous, are giving legitimacy to the bigotry associated with them.

For most political memes, it is clear that they are representing the opinions of the individuals who created them, and those opinions are often presented as fact. Of particular concern are political memes that contain verifiably false information. An illustrative example can be found in a meme that circulated widely on social media upon Trump entering the Republican primary. The meme featured a picture of a younger-looking Trump with a quotation supposedly attributed to a 1998 interview given to *People* magazine:

> If I were to run [for president], I'd run as a Republican. They're the dumbest group of voters in the country. They believe anything on Fox

News. I could lie and they'd still eat it up. I bet my numbers would be terrific

It did not take fact checkers long to verify that Trump had not given such a statement to *People* magazine in 1998, nor had he ever publicly said anything similar (Lacapria, 2017). Yet the meme went viral on social media because it presented a caricature of Trump that liberals wanted to believe.

Perhaps the most pedagogically worrisome types of memes are those that appear to be reporting objective facts. Consider, for example, the meme in Figure 7.2; it was shared widely on social media in the midst of Congressional Republicans' first failed attempt at repealing and replacing the Affordable Care Act, colloquially known as Obamacare, in 2017.

Although the 8 million figure is incorrect,[4] what makes this meme particularly problematic is that it actually reports some accurate data from the nonpartisan Congressional Budget Office (CBO) analysis on the Republicans' repeal and replace plan. The CBO did posit that the Republican plan would lead to 24 million uninsured (although they did not claim those individuals would die)—by 2026 (Congressional Budget Office, 2017). The meme, however, conveniently fails to state that the CBO analysis is a projection over time and insinuates that their analysis is an indication of what would happen immediately should the legislation be passed.

This meme, based on inaccurate statistics and a misrepresentation of the CBO report, was circulated widely on social media and was used as evidence by conservatives that the CBO report was "fake news." It only takes a couple of minutes of Googling to completely debunk the premise of the meme. Yet many people chose to simply retweet or hit "share," which is illustrative of the psychology behind political memes and why they are effective in shaping public opinion.

WHY POLITICAL MEMES ARE EFFECTIVE

Psychologically speaking, memes are near-perfect vehicles for reinforcing users' preexisting opinions. They are usually short and pithy, making them easy to read and process. Due to the already self-reinforcing atmosphere of most users' social media feeds (Knobloch-Westerwick, 2012; Slater, 2015), individuals will generally not have the motivation to think critically about the points presented in a given meme (Kunda, 1990; Lodge & Taber, 2013; Lord, Ross, & Lepper, 1979).

Political psychologists Drew Westen, Pavel Blagov, Keith Harenski, Clint Kilts, and Stephan Hamann (2006) found that hearing agreeable political information is related to activity in the brain's pleasure centers while disagreeable information is related to activity in areas related to punishment and pain. In other words, political information, such as that found

Figure 7.2. Affordable Care Act Repeal Meme

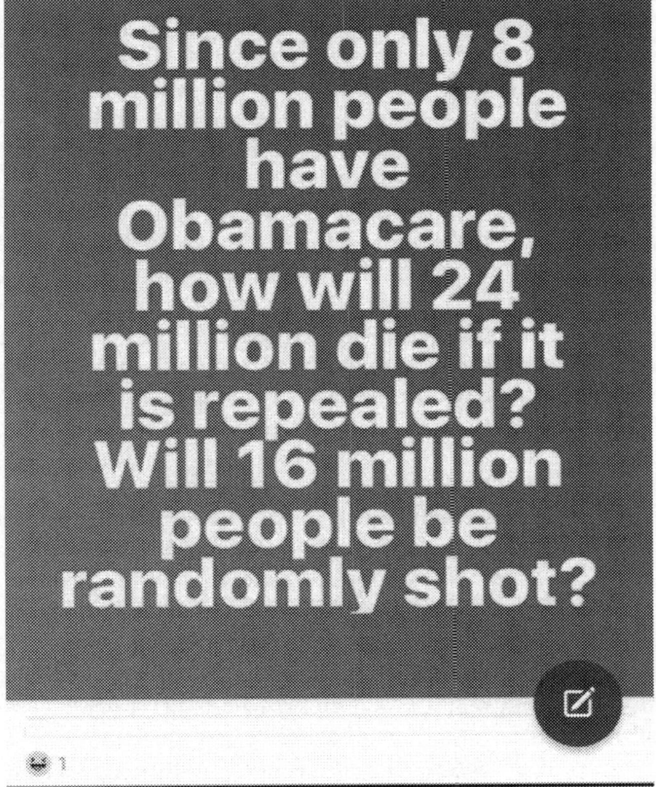

Grand Ol Math

in memes, tends to activate the emotional centers of the brain in people with partisan preferences. Further, encountering pro- and counterattitudinal information generally impacts people's feelings about political in- and out-groups (Garrett et al., 2014).

Memes reinforce positive feelings for groups the user identifies with and promote negative feelings toward opposing groups. When an individual experiences identity threat (a challenge to their self-concept, beliefs, or values) they are likely to seek to bolster their self-esteem. As psychologists Steven Fein and Steven Spencer (1997) found, such ego boosts are often accomplished through derogating out-groups, usually relying on stereotypes and other negative images. Given that memes are often used to mock or delegitimize political opponents (Ross & Rivers, 2017), individuals reading attitude-consistent memes will likely receive an ego boost from doing so.

Group identification is also one of the primary forces driving users to share memes. Sharing memes fulfills a social function. One key way to build and reinforce bonds among individuals is through sharing emotions (Peters & Kashima, 2007). As encountering memes is mostly an emotional experience, sharing memes amounts to a digital version of sharing one's feelings. By posting a meme to one's social media feed, one is sending a public signal of one's political beliefs and reinforcing social bonds among members of the same group.[5]

The stronger the affective response to a meme, the more likely the meme is to be shared. A study on viral videos by social psychologists Rosanna Guadagno, Daniel Rempala, Shannon Murphy, and Bradley Okdie (2013) found that videos that received the strongest affective response were the most likely to be shared. Interestingly, their study found that negative affective responses were also likely to be shared if the source of the post was perceived to be an out-group member.

For example, prior to the 2016 election, Donald Trump, Jr., tweeted a meme (Figure 7.3) comparing refugees from Syria to a bowl of Skittles with three poisoned pieces. While the tweet was likely designed to signal support for antirefugee policies to the Republican base, it also generated a storm of controversy, subsequently leading to news coverage and countermemes quoting the original meme. The outrage generated by the meme served to reinforce the group identity of those who supported accepting Syrian refugees while the meme itself reinforced the conservative opposition.

These events are consistent with a phenomenon observed in a multiwave panel study by Garrett et al. (2014) wherein respondents who viewed pro-party information simultaneously with counterparty information became more affectively polarized (see Iyengar, Sood, & Lelkes, 2012).

Though the popularity and sharing of memes has little to do with factual persuasion, their very ubiquity can have a (mis)informative effect. Repeating a claim, regardless of whether it is true, increases the likelihood that claim will be believed. In studies of the *illusory truth effect*, researchers have found that participants view claims they have previously heard as more credible (Hasher, Goldstein, & Toppino, 1977; Unkelbach & Rom, 2017). Even when participants have some knowledge about a topic, the repetition of false information can increase doubts (Fazio, Brashier, Payne, & Marsh, 2015).

Once misleading or false information is present in a person's mind, it is difficult to counteract. Attempts at correcting misinformation can even backfire (Nyhan & Reifler, 2010), resulting in a person becoming more entrenched in the false belief. When a false belief supports an individual's preexisting biases or identity, corrections are even more likely to produce a backfire effect (Jarman, 2016). In short, memes are effective because they appeal to users' preexisting beliefs, provide a vehicle for strengthening group identification and bonds through sharing, and plant ideas in users' minds that are difficult to counteract.

Figure 7.3. Meme Shared by Donald Trump, Jr., During the 2016 Presidential Campaign

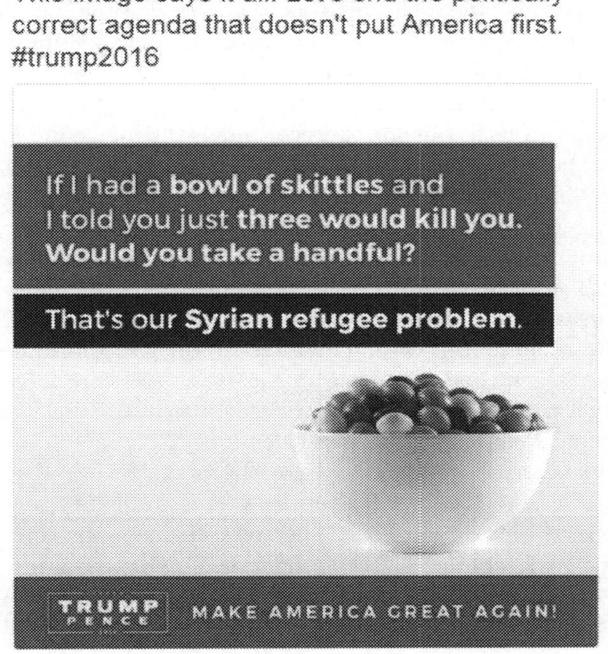

TEACHING ABOUT POLITICAL MEMES AND THE LIMITS OF MEDIA LITERACY

The influential nature of political memes makes them worthy of studying as part of a 21st-century civic education. However, memes do not necessarily lend themselves to traditional media literacy instruction. Consider, for example, the most recent position statement on media literacy by the National Council for the Social Studies (NCSS) (2016). Among the key questions that NCSS suggests teachers have their students ask when analyzing media messages are the following:

- Who paid for [the media]?
- Who made this message?
- Why was [this media] made?
- When was [this media] made?

- Where or how was it shared with the public?
- Is [this media] fact, opinion, or something else?
- What are the sources of the information, ideas, or assertions? (pp. 183–184)

Memes do not offer clear answers to any of these questions. They have no bylines or timestamps, and by the time students encounter them, they will have been shared by an untold number of social media users. It is also usually difficult to tell if a meme is reporting fact or opinion given that they rarely have citations to outside sources, and as the meme in Figure 7.2 illustrates, even those that appear to report facts may be sharing inaccurate data or misrepresenting factual information to fit a certain narrative.

How, then, should teachers broach political memes in their classrooms? Simply dismissing them as the byproducts of a digital media age in which anyone with a social media account can posit political opinions online ignores the impact that memes have on political discourse in the United States. Yet treating them as one would treat traditional media outlets may send the message that memes should be considered legitimate forms of political media, which would further blur the lines between fact and opinion that has come to define American politics in recent years.

To help students understand both the prevalence and importance of political memes, we suggest that teachers have students approach political memes from a political psychology perspective, as opposed to a traditional media literacy standpoint. The remainder of this chapter outlines three basic steps that teachers can take to illustrate the ease by which political memes are created and how they validate people's preexisting political beliefs.

Exploring How Political Memes Are Created and Shared

With traditional media literacy instruction, students approach a news source with a healthy degree of skepticism about inherent bias but are inclined to believe that a news source is legitimate until proven otherwise. With political memes, students should take the opposite approach. Given that anyone with access to the Internet can create memes, students should approach any political meme with an assumption that it was created using incorrect or misinterpreted facts and designed with the express purpose of promoting a specific agenda.

One way to start this conversation is to have students create a political meme of their own. While it is possible that some students will have experience creating memes, and even political memes, many students may not have a true understanding of how easy they are to create. Anyone with basic digital media skills can create a meme, and even students who have never attempted one will be able to quickly learn the process.

A Google search for "meme generator" derives dozens of websites offering free meme-generating software. Once students decide on the political message they want to make and identify images and text that will help them articulate that message, it only takes a few clicks before they can create a meme that could be shared on social media. So as not to encourage the spread of misinformation or vitriol online, teachers should make sure that students' messages are grounded in verifiable information and avoid inappropriate stereotypes of race, class, gender, or any other social group.

Seeing the relative ease by which political memes can be created should alert students to the fact that any political memes that they see in their social media feeds should be taken with a grain of salt. However, to really have students understand the way political memes influence political discourse, teachers could have students upload their memes to their own social media accounts. While some schools and districts may have rules that prohibit social media use at school, students could easily complete this assignment at home if needed. It may be advisable, however, for teachers to seek permission from parents and administrators before initiating this step of the assignment. Any sort of political meme uploaded to social media, even a meme grounded in fact, could lead to intolerant comments from other users, and some parents may not want their children engaged in such discourse online. In addition, teachers should also set expectations for students' online decorum, especially if they receive negative feedback on their meme.

After students post their memes, they could then track the number of likes, shares/retweets, and comments that they receive over a certain period of time (e.g., a week). They could also experiment with the various privacy settings on Facebook and Twitter to see what differences occurred, if any, when the posts were made public versus just shared within their established social networks. In addition, students could track the following:

- What types of people shared/liked the meme? (e.g., friends, family, friends of friends, complete strangers)
- Were there any trends associated with the people who shared/liked the meme? (e.g., age, race/ethnicity, known political affiliation)
- From a geographic standpoint, how far did their meme reach? (e.g., different states or countries)

At the end of the exercise, students could report back and compare how their memes fared in comparison with those of their peers. Assuming differences exist, students could then compare memes to see if the memes that had more shares/likes had similar qualities. Such information could help students identify how fast political memes can spread and what types of political memes gain the most traction online (e.g., positive memes versus negative memes).

Understanding Meme Messaging

Once students have an idea of how easily memes are created and spread, it is important for them to be able to evaluate political memes that come across their social media feeds. Here, some traditional media literacy strategies can be used to help students understand the type of messaging strategies that are used in political memes. Turning again to the NCSS (2016) position statement on media literacy, the following questions could be used to guide students' evaluation of political memes:

- Who might benefit from this message?
- Who might be harmed by it?
- Why might this message matter to me?
- What is this [meme] about (and what makes you think that)?
- What ideas, values, information, and/or points of view are overt? Implied?
- What is left out of this message that might be important to know?
- What techniques are used?
- How might different people understand this message differently?
- What is my interpretation of this [meme] and what do I learn about myself from my reaction or interpretation? (pp. 183–184)

Consider, for example, the Skittles meme depicted in Figure 7.3. It is clear that the subject of the meme is the issue of granting asylum to Syrian refugees, a position Clinton supported but Trump did not. Although there is no way to know for sure who created the meme (the tagline wants the reader to think it was created by the Trump campaign), the fact that Donald Trump, Jr. tweeted it suggests that the message was favorable to Trump and, conversely, potentially damaging to Clinton.

Such a simplistic reading of the meme, however, misses the more nuanced political messages being sent. While the specific focus of the meme is Syrian refugees, the implied message is alerting Americans to the dangers of immigration and letting "others" into our borders. This meme suggests that the world is a dangerous place and that there are groups that would love to infiltrate the United States to cause American citizens harm.

The technique being used in this meme is fear mongering. It is certainly possible that if the United States admitted Syrian refugees, there could be a few that intended to commit acts of terror or other crimes. Yet the size of the bowl of Skittles depicted in the meme implies that the average American would have a good chance of being harmed by the small number of refugees who might enter the United States with violent intentions.

The meme does not give any information about the total number of Syrian refugees versus the small number with violent intentions, nor does it provide any nuance about the process of allowing immigrants of any kind into the United States. In reality, any Syrian refugees who were to enter the United States would first have to go through a rigorous vetting process. Research also shows that the average likelihood of an American citizen being killed by an immigrant-linked terrorist attack is roughly one in 3.6 million. When applied specifically to refugees, the odds jump to one in 3.6 billion (Beauchamp, 2017).

In other words, for the meme to provide an accurate representation of the risks associated with admitting Syrian refugees into the United States, the bowl of Skittles would have needed to be much larger—approximately as big as an Olympic-size swimming pool. Of course, even if the meme had presented a Skittles bowl that would have accurately represented the odds of being killed by a Syrian refugee, the threat of violence from a Syrian refugee would still be present, and research has shown that people are prone to irrational assessments of events or risks that are statistically insignificant if they play upon stereotypes or fears (e.g., Slovic, 1987).

Understanding the Political Psychology of Memes

Assume for a moment that Donald Trump, Jr., had tweeted a meme that contained the same message, but the size of the bowl of Skittles was proportional to the actual risk of being harmed by a Syrian refugee. Chances are, the meme would have had the same effect. Those who hold irrational fears about terrorism or possess xenophobic attitudes toward Middle Eastern immigrants could have easily come to the same conclusion that letting in Syrian refugees was a risk that the United States did not need to take. The level of risk likely would not have made much of a difference.

Therefore, it is not surprising that the original meme went viral. It played to the fears and stereotypes that many Trump voters held about terrorism, immigrants, and border security prior to the Syrian refugee crisis. In other words, this meme likely did not change minds as much as it reinforced preexisting views. As already noted, affirming values and beliefs is a primary function of political memes, and it is important for students to recognize how effective memes are at achieving this goal.

One way students could better understand the psychology behind memes is to track the political memes that they see on their social media feeds and answer the following questions:

- Are the comments generated by the meme ideologically consistent?
- Do the comments generated by the meme serve to affirm the message represented in the meme?
- What occurs if someone questions or attempts to disprove the message in the meme? Are they attacked or does it lead to a fact-based discussion?

It is likely that students will see that most people post political memes that correspond to their preexisting ideological beliefs. The messages presented by the meme (and thus the poster's preexisting ideological beliefs) are then reinforced by the social media echo chambers that most people have created for themselves, and any dissent is immediately attacked or dismissed. If students see this same pattern occur both in their own social media feeds and across those of their classmates, they should be able to recognize that the primary function of political memes is ideological, not informational.

Overall, our strategy for approaching memes in the classroom aims to give students practice in more intentional thinking about this relatively new form of political communication. Because memes rely on the quick but bias-prone emotion- and identity-based parts of cognition, it is beneficial for teachers to build up slower, more systematic thinking habits regarding memes (see Kahneman, 2011).

This approach is similar to Kahne and Bowyer's (2017) findings about the efficacy of instruction on determining the trustworthiness of online sources and evaluating evidence in reducing ideologically biased evaluations of political cartoons. If students can understand the basic creation and functioning of memes, they should be better equipped to view them with healthy amounts of skepticism.

CONCLUSION

Political memes are an influential part of 21st-century American political discourse. Although teachers should not treat them in the same manner as traditional forms of media, dismissing memes entirely from discussions of political media would be a mistake. Today's students are likely to encounter political memes more often than traditional news outlets; therefore, it is essential that they understand the purpose of political memes and learn to think critically about the messages that they portray.

NOTES

1. Although we are focusing on examples from the United States, memes have influenced politics in other nations as well. See, for example, Piata (2016) and Martinez-Rolan and Pineiro-Otero (2016).

2. Occasionally, however, memes can help boost a politician's image. Communications scholars Karrin Anderson and Kristina Sheeler (2014), for example, have argued that the "Texts from Hillary" memes that depicted the then-Secretary of State wearing sunglasses and making snarky texts to other politicians and notable celebrities helped Clinton rebound from an embarrassing primary loss in 2008.

3. While most memes associated with race, gender, sexuality, and religion are divisive, occasionally they can be used as a way for traditionally marginalized groups to form a collective identity. See Gal, Shifman, and Kampf (2016) for an example.

4. According to figures at the start of 2017, over 11 million people had signed up for the Affordable Care Act (Luhby, 2017).

5. While our focus here is on political groups, memes can build bonds among any salient social group. See Gal et al. (2016) for a description of how the "It gets better" memes were used to construct a collective identity among LGBTQ users.

REFERENCES

Anderson, K. V., & Sheeler, K. H. (2014). Texts (and tweets) from Hillary: Meta-meming and postfeminist political culture. *Presidential Studies Quarterly, 44*, 224–243.

Beauchamp, Z. (2017, June 26). You're more likely to be killed by your own clothes than by an immigrant terrorist. *Vox.* Retrieved from www.vox.com/2016/9/13/12901950/terrorism-immigrants-clothes

Congressional Budget Office. (2017, March 13). American health care act. Retrieved from www.cbo.gov/publication/52486

Dawkins, R. (1976). *The selfish gene.* Oxford, United Kingdom: Oxford University Press.

Fazio, L. K., Brashier, N. M., Payne, B. K., & Marsh, E. J. (2015). Knowledge does not protect against illusory truth. *Journal of Experimental Psychology, 144*, 993–1002.

Fein, S., & Spencer, S. J. (1997). Prejudice as self-image maintenance: Affirming the self through derogating others. *Journal of Personality and Social Psychology, 73*, 31–44.

Gal, N., Shifman, L., & Kampf, Z. (2016). "It gets better": Internet memes and the construction of collective identity. *New Media & Society, 18*, 1698–1714.

Garrett, R. K., Gvirsman, S. D., Johnson, B. K., Tsfati, Y., Neo, R., & Dal, A. (2014). Implications of pro- and counterattitudinal information exposure for affective polarization. *Human Communication Research, 40*, 309–332.

Guadagno, R. E., Rempala, D. M., Murphy, S., & Okdie, B. M. (2013). What makes a video go viral? An analysis of emotional contagion and Internet memes. *Computers in Human Behavior, 29*, 2312–2319.

Hasher, L., Goldstein, D., & Toppino, T. (1977). Frequency and the conference of referential validity. *Journal of Verbal Learning and Verbal Behavior, 16*, 107–112.

Huntington, H. E. (2016). Pepper spray cop and the American dream: Using synecdoche and metaphor to unlock Internet memes' visual political rhetoric. *Communication Studies, 67*, 77–93.

Iyengar, S., Sood, G., & Lelkes, Y. (2012). Affect, not ideology: A social identity perspective on polarization. *Public Opinion Quarterly, 76*, 405–431.

Jarman, J. W. (2016). Influence of political affiliation and criticism on the effectiveness of political fact-checking. *Communication Research Reports, 33*, 9–15.

Journell, W. (2011). Teachers' controversial issue decisions related to race, gender, and religion during the 2008 presidential election. *Theory & Research in Social Education, 39*, 348–392.

Journell, W. (Ed.). (2016). *Teaching social issues in an era of divisiveness: The challenges of discussing social issues in a non-partisan way.* Lanham, MD: Rowman & Littlefield.

Journell, W. (2017). *Teaching politics in secondary education: Engaging with contentious issues*. Albany, NY: State University of New York Press.

Kahne, J., & Bowyer, B. (2017). Educating for democracy in a partisan age: Confronting the challenges of motivated reasoning and misinformation. *American Educational Research Journal*, *54*, 3–34.

Kahneman, D. (2011) *Thinking, fast and slow*. New York, NY: Farrar, Strauss, & Giroux.

Knobel, M., & Lankshear, C. (2007). Online memes, affinities, and cultural production. In M. Knobel & C. Lankshear (Eds.), *A new literacies sampler* (pp. 199–228). New York, NY: Peter Lang.

Knobloch-Westerwick, S. (2012). Selective exposure and reinforcement of attitudes and partisanship before a presidential election. *Journal of Communication, 62*, 628–642.

Kunda, Z. (1990). The case for motivated reasoning. *Psychological Bulletin*, *108*, 480–498.

Lacapria, K. (2017, November 30). Did Donald Trump say Republicans are the "dumbest group of voters"? *Snopes*. Retrieved from www.snopes.com/fact-check/1998-trump-people-quote/

Lodge, M., & Taber, C. (2013). *The rationalizing voter*. New York, NY: Cambridge University Press.

Lord, C. G., Ross, L., & Lepper, M. R. (1979). Biased assimilation and attitude polarization: The effects of prior theories on subsequently considered evidence. *Journal of Personality and Social Psychology*, *37*, 2098–2109.

Luhby, T. (2017, January 10). Obamacare remains popular, with 11.5 million sign ups so far. *CNN Business*. Retrieved from money.cnn.com/2017/01/10/news/economy/obamacare-enrollment/index.html

Martinez-Rolan, X., & Pineiro-Otero, T. (2016). The use of memes in the discourse of political parties on Twitter: Analysing the 2015 state of the nation debate. *Communications & Society, 29*, 145–159.

Melber, A. (2012, October 17). Why Romney is losing the meme election. *The Nation*. Retrieved from www.thenation.com/article/why-romney-losing-meme-election/

Milner, R. M. (2013). Pop polyvocality: Internet memes, public participation, and the Occupy Wall Street movement. *International Journal of Communication, 7*, 2357–2390.

National Council for the Social Studies (NCSS). (2016). Media literacy. *Social Education, 80*, 183–185.

Nyhan, B., & Reifler, J. (2010). When corrections fail: The persistence of political misperceptions. *Political Behavior*, *32*, 303–330.

Peters, K., & Kashima, Y. (2007). From social talk to social action: Shaping the social triad with emotion sharing. *Journal of Personality and Social Psychology*, *93*, 780–797.

Piata, A. (2016). When metaphor becomes a joke: Metaphor journeys from political ads to Internet memes. *Journal of Pragmatics, 106*, 39–56.

Ross, A. S., & Rivers, D. J. (2017). Digital cultures of political participation: Internet memes and the discursive delegitimization of the 2016 U.S. Presidential candidates. *Discourse, Context and Media*, *16*, 1–11.

Schwartz, H. (2015, February 13). "Thanks Obama." The evolution of a meme that defined a presidency. *The Washington Post*. Retrieved from www.washingtonpost.com/news/the-fix/wp/2015/02/13/thanks-obama-the-evolution-of-a-meme-that-defined-a-presidency/

Shifman, L. (2014). *Memes in digital culture*. Cambridge, MA: Massachusetts Institute of Technology Press.

Slater, M. D. (2015). Reinforcing spirals model: Conceptualizing the relationship between media content exposure and the development and maintenance of attitudes. *Media Psychology, 18*, 370–395.

Slovic, P. (1987). Perception of risk. *Science, 236*, 280–285.

Tay, G. (2015). Binders full of LOLitics: Political humour, Internet memes, and play in the 2012 US presidential election (and beyond). *European Journal of Humour Research, 2*(4), 46–73.

Unkelbach, C., & Rom, S. C. (2017). A referential theory of the repetition-induced truth effect. *Cognition, 160*, 110–126.

Westen, D., Blagov, P. S., Harenski, K., Kilts, C., & Hamann, S. (2006). Neural bases of motivated reasoning: an FMRI study of emotional constraints on partisan political judgment in the 2004 U.S. presidential election. *Journal of Cognitive Neuroscience, 18*, 1947–1958.

Wiggins, B. E., & Bowers, G. B. (2015). Memes as genre: A structurational analysis of the memescape. *New Media & Society, 17*, 1886-1906.

Williams, R. (1999). "Kilroy was here," "Where's the beef?" and "Marlboro man": A memetic insight for organizational development. *Organization Development Journal, 17*, 113–118.

Yoon, I. (2016). Why is it not just a joke? Analysis of Internet memes associated with racism and hidden ideology of colorblindness. *Journal of Cultural Research in Art Education, 33*, 92–123.

CHAPTER 8

Two Truths and Fake News

Lessons for Young Learners

Jennifer Hauver

Dinner has just ended and there is a flurry of activity in my kitchen. Plates being cleared, water running, lunches being prepared for school tomorrow. My girls, ages 14 and 11, continue the conversation that began over spaghetti and meatballs: The all-important update on "who likes whom" at the middle school.

Sarah, my older daughter, announces to all within earshot that her sister, Grace, likes one of the neighbor boys, Adam. "Do not!" Grace yells, turning red in the face. "Taylor says you make googly eyes at him on the bus. She even says you want him to ask you to the winter dance," Sarah jests. "Guess what, Sarah?" Grace retorts: "Fake news."

I look up from the dishwasher. "What did you say?"

"Fake news. Not. True."

Sarah zips up her lunch bag. "Maybe. Or maybe it IS true and you just don't want it reported." She winks, and Grace lets out a frustrated scream, then turns to chase her sister out of the room.

When, I wonder, did fake news become adolescent-speak? But there it was. And so aptly appropriated.

Our children may have adopted the term, but do they really know fake news when they see it? As a young girl, I can remember standing in the grocery store checkout line looking up at magazine racks filled with various and sundry publications. The *National Enquirer* always caught my eye. "Elvis is back!" the cover would scream. "Two-headed baby born in Indiana!" My eyes wide, I would ask my mother about what I saw. She would simply roll her eyes and tell me not to believe everything I read. "Why would they print it if it wasn't true?" I would ask. "Just trying to sell newspapers," she would reply, "People like to be entertained."

Today, fake news is harder to spot because it is rarely intended to entertain. Its creators intend it to blend in, masquerading as legitimate. Fake news is intended to incite discord, shake our faith in government, and even sway elections. Cambridge Dictionary (2018) tells us that *fake news* is: "false stories that appear to be news, spread on the Internet or using other media, usually created to influence political views or as a joke" (para. 1). The fakeness of fake news is subtle—only a critical consumer can spot it.

Even I struggle to navigate my way through the myriad news stories that bombard my phone, my doorstep, and my television set every day. I work to follow evidence trails and corroborate stories across sources. However, I must admit, I do not always know what to believe. I want to trust that those in the media and politics are acting ethically, but I do not always. I bounce between sadness at my own cynicism and pride in my healthy skepticism that keeps me alert and engaged. The amount of news and the pace at which it comes at us can be overwhelming. Being an informed citizen requires new sets of skills.

Sadly, a recent study by the Stanford History Education Group (McGrew, Breakstone, Ortega, Smith, & Wineburg, 2018) revealed that we are ill-equipped to reason our way through the constant barrage of information we encounter. More than 80% of middle schoolers, for example, tasked with identifying advertisements on a news website believed that "native" advertising (i.e., advertising embedded in the page) was news. Less than 20% of high schoolers, when asked to evaluate a photograph as a source of evidence, asked where the photo had come from. Forty percent stated that they believed the photo was a trustworthy source of information about an event simply because it appeared to have been taken at the scene. Even college-age students who were asked to analyze a tweet rarely noted the source of the tweet or considered the importance of the political agendas of those behind the posts.

Online reasoning and media literacy are essential skills for navigating our information-rich world. Fortunately, more educators are making it a priority to help students develop these skills. The National Council for the Social Studies (NCSS, 2016) put forth a position statement on media literacy, asserting: "Social studies educators should provide young people with the awareness and abilities to critically question and create new media and technology—essential skills for active citizenship in our democracy" (p. 183).

The recently developed *C3 Framework* designed to accompany state social studies standards focuses on critical literacy skills (NCSS, 2013). Even our nonprofit and media partners, like those at the Newseum, PBS and *The New York Times,* are creating online and face-to-face workshops for educators and students to help outsmart online trolls. I am inspired by the collective responsibility we are taking for educating ourselves and our young people; yet the most important interventions, particularly for young learners, occur in the classroom.

In what follows, I share eight minilessons I have developed for elementary and middle school children aimed at honing their skills as critical consumers of text. They are lessons that I have implemented in elementary and middle school classrooms with teacher partners in Georgia and Virginia. In each, I have tried to include suggestions for adapting to a range of ages. I believe that even young children understand there are two sides to every story and are hungry for tools for deciding which story to believe, or reaching an understanding that incorporates both sides as versions of a single experience. Of course, teaching these skills looks different when working with emerging readers than it does with middle schoolers conducting research projects. I leave it to the reader to determine how best to make the ideas presented work for their specific setting.

TWO TRUTHS AND FAKE NEWS: WHAT MAKES SOMETHING TRUE?

This first minilesson is a spin-off of a well-rehearsed ice-breaker game: "Two Truths and a Lie." In this game, all the players write down or say three things about themselves: two of them true, one a lie. It is up to the other members of the group to correctly guess which is which.

The minilesson begins the same way. I ask children to write down (or say) three things about themselves; two of them are true, and one is "fake news." I then invite them to play the game in table groups, trying to guess which claims are true. My first goal is to have students differentiate between what they believe to be true and untrue. I ask them to tell us which statements are which.

My second goal is to have students explain what makes one claim true and another "fake." Together, we might generate a list of criteria for claims that are true. For instance, there might be a document that "proves" it, others who can confirm it, or others who saw it or experienced it themselves.

Imagine that Miguel writes: "I have one sister. My family speaks Spanish at home. I like basketball." Miguel can "prove" that he only has one sister. There are documents to prove that fact. Further, his parents would say he is telling the truth. They would also confirm that the family speaks Spanish at home. These initial criteria can be useful in assessing the claims of others we read.

For older students, I push a bit further. I want them to think about the subtleties of language. According to Miguel, his third statement, "I like basketball," is fake because he actually loves to play soccer. I might ask Miguel whether he likes basketball at all? Would it be more accurate to say that he does not prefer basketball, or that he does not like to play basketball, but he does like to watch others play?

The probing questions can extend to the truths as well. If, for example, Miguel had two sisters, would the first statement be mostly true or mostly fake? If his family also speaks English at home, does that make the second sentence untrue? My goal is not to have students distrust language. Rather, I want them to use language carefully and read it critically. I want them to realize that vague and sloppy use of language can blur the lines between real and fake.

THE DATA SPEAK FOR THEMSELVES: INTERPRETING DATA

As an extension of "Two Truths and Fake News," this minilesson has students interpreting data, generating true and fake claims. As students walk into the room, I give each one a sticky note and ask them to answer the question on the board. Perhaps the question is "How did you get to school today?" Students can write down or draw a picture of their mode of transportation (e.g., walking, bus, car, bike).

We then work together to construct a graph at the front of the room representing all students' data. After all the students have posted their information, I gather the children in front of the graph and ask them to help me interpret the data. Next to the graph, I write "What can we say?"

Together, we generate statements that *could be true* based on the data before us. Maya suggests, "More children ride the bus than take a car to school." Good, I say, but more children where? Are we talking about all children? Everywhere in the world?

She revises her claim: "More children in our class ride the bus to school than take a car." Better, I say. It is more specific and more accurate given the data we have. We write as many claims as we can, and I ask students to compare how different claims tell slightly different stories. For instance, we could say, "More children ride the bus to school than take the car." We could also say, "The majority of students in the class walk to school." Both of these claims are true given the data we have, but they focus on different things.

With older, more advanced children, I even try to get them to stretch the truth as far as possible. If I believed, for instance, that children should get lots of exercise and that the best way to get to school is to walk, I might say, "Eight of the 22 children in the class fail to get adequate exercise in the morning." The purpose here is to see how data can be manipulated for persuasive purposes.

I also use this opportunity to get students to think about the temporality of data. I might ask them to imagine what would happen to our data set if three more children joined our class or if two children in our class moved closer to the school. Is it possible that our data could change over time? What if tomorrow Liza goes to the dentist in the morning and her mom drops her off at school rather than having her walk? The results may be different tomorrow. Our data set represents a specific time and place. So, understanding the context of data collected matters.

A final line of inquiry focuses on the question itself. If I had asked the question differently, I would likely have gotten different answers. What if I had said, "How do you usually get to school?" Teachers could spend as little or as long as they want on this conversation depending on their goals and the students they are teaching. For me, what is important is that students are not allowed to be intellectually lazy, taking language or data at face value.

SAVVY CONSUMER: ANALYZING AUTHOR INTENTION

I designed this third minilesson on analyzing author intention for upper elementary students. If I were working with younger students, I would focus my attention on familiar advertisements, projecting one or two in front of the class, and talking about its purpose and audience. For those in 3rd grade and up, I include a variety of materials and have students read them individually.

As students come into the classroom, they are greeted with a variety of texts: piles of newspaper and magazine clippings, websites on computer screens, brochures, and pamphlets. I invite them to peruse the materials and look for something that interests them. I then ask students to tell the class what type of document they have chosen. I am interested to see what language children will use to describe the text in front of them (e.g., "news," "commercial," "it's facts," "it's information," "it's a story"). I write these descriptors on the board—something we will come back to at the close of the lesson.

I then distribute a worksheet to each child and tell them that they will now analyze their text. They must do the best they can to answer the questions on the sheet:

- Who created this text?
- What do we know about who created it?
- What is the author trying to accomplish with the text?
- How do you know?
- What clues exist in the text or around the text to help us understand its purpose?
- Who is the audience for this text?
- Again, how do you know?
- What clues exist in and around the text to help us understand its audience?

I invite students to get together into groups of three to share their texts and analyses. I tell them that when they have finished, they should be ready to report out two things:

- What they think the author of the text is trying to do
- Whether they have changed their mind about what the text is

As students share, many amend their initial guesses about what the text is (e.g., "I thought this was a news article, but it's really just someone's opinion.") Sometimes the author is not clear or the message is confusing (e.g., "I thought this was just facts, but it seems one-sided. Maybe the author is trying to convince me rather than just report facts.") I remind students that every text has an author and that we must always ask ourselves what that author is trying to accomplish. This attention to detail is an important part of being a careful and critical reader.

LET'S GET SOME PERSPECTIVE! AUTHOR PERSPECTIVE AND CORROBORATION

The purpose of this minilesson is to help students wrestle with authorship and perspective. Rather than assuming that when two accounts differ one is true and one is fake, I want them to think about the possibility that two people who experienced the same event might tell different stories about it. For younger children, I might use a book like *Duck! Rabbit!* (Rosenthal & Lichtenheld, 2009) or *The Important Book* (Brown & Weisgard, 1999).

In the first book, two narrators argue over whether the drawing before them is a duck or a rabbit, both laying out reasonable arguments for their interpretation. This text is useful for highlighting perspective. I have followed this reading up with opportunities for children to interpret abstract drawings and talking about their reasons. *The Important Book* is filled with statements about what makes various things important: snow, rain, a spoon. Children can agree or disagree with the author and even generate their own versions of the text, discussing their different perspectives about what makes things important to them.

For older children, I not only want them to understand that people have different opinions, but I also want them to think about why—in the news—people may tell different stories about the same event. Certainly, there are the practical matters—people have different vantage points, perhaps. However, they also may have different levels of investment in an experience or approach an experience with different purposes.

I look for examples in the news of two competing stories about an event. Take a political rally, for instance. People may attend a rally in support of its cause. They may also attend a rally because they oppose it. They arrive at the scene with different purposes and beliefs. Is it any wonder that they will have different stories to tell of their experience there?

I want students to recognize that difference in reporting does not necessarily make one version true. This fact does not mean, however, that any version is as good as any other. In addition to considering who the authors of a source are so that we can assess their perspectives, we also have the tool of corroboration. It is likely, that even in two very different stories, we might find common pieces. So, after reading the documents initially in search of what is different, this time we read with an eye to what is the same. Doing so helps us to determine what is more likely "fact" (time of day, location) and what is opinion.

INTERVIEW WITH A JOURNALIST

One of the more exciting minilessons I have been able to conduct with students is having them interview a real live, practicing journalist, in this case a woman. I implemented this lesson in a middle school classroom, but it could be easily adapted to any age. Before our guest speaker arrived, I invited the children to generate a list of questions with me, things we wondered about how a journalist does her work:

- How does she find her sources?
- How does she check her information?
- How does she know whom to trust?
- When does she know that she's done looking?
- How does she decide which side of a story to tell?
- Is it necessary to balance a story out?
- Are both sides always worthy of equal representation?
- What is the most interesting story she's researched? What made it so?

We also selected a couple of articles written by the journalist that we wanted to ask her to discuss. Having specific stories in mind, I believed, would help our guest get specific with her answers. We typed up our list of questions, and I sent them to our guest in advance of her visit. When she arrived, I asked her to start by talking to us about how she got into journalism and what she likes about her job. I then asked the students to pose their questions, one at a time.

I told students that they should listen for the specific skills and tools our guest employs to tell the most accurate story she can. They would be using these tools themselves in creating a class newsletter, and they would need to be ready to defend their process, just as she did. Once our guest left, we reflected on our time with her and generated a list of lessons we learned. My goal here was not to turn each of my students into a journalist. Rather, I hoped to help them construct a robust understanding of how "real" news is produced—news that can be substantiated and corroborated, news that is transparent and, when necessary, tentative in its reporting.

DIGGING BELOW THE SURFACE: FOLLOWING EVIDENCE TRAILS

In our busy lives, it is tempting to read a headline, followed perhaps by a short blurb underneath, and think we have gotten the news. We can scroll through the updates on our phone and feel relatively "in the know." If we have the time and the inclination, we might actually click the link and read the corresponding story. Rarely does even the most thoughtful consumer of the news go much further.

Yet, not digging below the surface to follow the evidence trail means we have abdicated our responsibility for checking our sources. We have, whether intentionally or not, decided to trust whatever information comes our way. It is important that we have the skills to dig when necessary. We need to be sure that we can check our own sources and confirm that we have trusted the right people.

To help develop these critical skills in young people, I invite them to find a piece of news that interests them. I begin by asking students to explain what about the piece they find interesting. I tell them that we are going to do our best to determine how trustworthy the source is. I ask them to read the piece in its entirety, trying to determine the main idea.

I then ask them to reread the piece, underlining the claims made by the authors and highlighting the evidence the authors includes in support of those claims. I ask students to share until I am sure that we understand some of the different ways that authors bolster their arguments (e.g., statistics, quotations, pointing to other examples of the same phenomenon).

We then move on to the next part of the dig. I ask students to outline one of the claims made by the authors and follow the evidence provided. They are free to go online and to the library to follow the trails (e.g., research studies provided, learning more about those interviewed or quoted). When we reconvene, we evaluate the reliability of the original sources, based on the reliability of the evidence provided. Some questions we ask might include the following:

- Do the authors deserve our trust?
- What have they done to earn it?
- Are they transparent about where they got their information?
- Are their sources reliable?
- How close to the issue/event were they?
- What biases might they have that would help explain their perspectives?
- If the reporting relies on research, who conducted that research and what did they find?

Though it will never be possible for us to dig beneath the surface of every article or follow every evidence trail, I want students to notice the ways that authors earn our trust. I want them to practice earning the trust of their readers, and I want them to trust themselves to determine what to believe and what not to believe.

ASK GOOGLE: DETERMINING A RELIABLE SOURCE

Young people are tech savvy. Yet we must not forget that though they spend inordinate amounts of time online, they do not necessarily know how to wade through what they find there. So often I hear teachers say that they send their students to Google something. I wonder, what then?

When my own children Google answers to homework problems, they tend to grab the first answer they can find, even if the source has a little box next to it indicating that it is an advertisement. They have been told not to trust Wikipedia, but that is the extent of the filter they have developed. In this minilesson I aim to help students determine what is a reliable online source. It is designed for upper-elementary and middle school students.

We start by choosing a single topic of interest to the class. It could be something related to a unit of study we are undertaking, or it could be a current event. I then ask students to open up their browsers and find a source they think is reliable related to our topic. Before they share with the class, I ask them to jot down some notes about what they think makes the source a good one:

- Which did they rule out automatically? Why?
- How far did they dig to determine if a source was reliable? What did they look for?

We brainstorm some criteria together. For example, more trustworthy sources tell us who the authors are. The authors tell us where they got their information. If someone paid for the publication, we know who. When we follow the evidence trails, we think the authors have accurately represented the information we find.

Once we have a list of criteria on the board, I ask students to look at their source again and decide if they still think it is reliable. If they need to, they can toss it back and keep looking. Once everyone has a source chosen, I ask for a few volunteers to share their source with the class. I put the source up on the class projector and we talk together about whether the source would be a good one to use for our class project.

As we talk, I remind students of the criteria on the board. Sometimes we must reject a source once we have analyzed it together, and I ask the students to keep digging for something better. Eventually, once we have a solid set of sources identified, we can get set to work answering our questions.

"I CAN'T HEAR YOU!": LISTENING WHEN YOU DON'T WANT TO

Ironically, despite the barrage of information flooding our inboxes and phones every day, we may be more isolated from true deliberation than we were before phones existed. The information we receive is filtered through software that picks up on our likes and dislikes, our ideological leanings, and our affiliations. More and more, we look for news that affirms our worldview, and more and more, that is exactly what we get.

Even young people choose which news sources will send them updates throughout the day. However, there is something lost when we insulate ourselves from dialogue across difference. We lose perspective, and we forget how to listen. In this important minilesson, my aim is to get students to sit with news stories that make them uncomfortable. The topic is not important to me nor, really, is the persuasion of the writer. What matters is that students select an article to read that asserts a position they do not believe to be right or true.[1]

Students might decide to read a piece on immigration from a news source they would not typically read (e.g., Fox News or National Public Radio). I ask them to read it first doing their best to withhold judgment. Then, I ask them to apply the same techniques they have been practicing to evaluate the reliability of the source.

I ask them to consider authorship, bias, evidence trails. I ask them to look for pieces they can possibly corroborate with other sources they know, and then I ask them to write a short reflection about what the piece contributes to their understanding of the issue. This reflection could be something they learned specifically about the issue itself or it could be something they learned about how different people frame the issue.

Once everyone has had a chance to read and reflect, we come together to discuss the value in reading news from a variety of sources. One thing I want students to understand is that staying within our own echo chamber can make us feel as if our way of understanding is the only way—or at least the only valid way. Pushing ourselves outside of our comfort zone, considering other points of view, builds understanding and respect. It may even lead to compromise and collective action. What is important to remember is that just because one may not like something, it does not mean it is "fake."

TOWARD CRITICAL HABITS OF MIND

Over the last year I have enjoyed piloting these lessons with teacher partners in a variety of settings. I am grateful for the opportunities I have had to refine my ideas in light of actual experience with engaged and beautifully surprising young people. Along the way, what has impressed me most has been students' deep thinking and their desire to understand. Their willingness to dig in has taught me a good deal about the need for this work and our continued commitment to develop effective methods for teaching critical literacy.

I have also learned much about what makes this work hard, namely, that doing this work well means taking the time to really engage in the process. The eight minilessons described here barely scratch the surface. To truly develop young people's habits of mind as critical consumers of text, we must make critical literacy skills a pillar of our work.

In the history classroom we can use primary documents as context for this work, examining author purpose, audience, context, corroborating to determine a "best" claim about the past. In reading classes we can practice the art of interrogating language, reading between the lines, and interpreting author intention. In writing classes we can apply our growing knowledge of technique to our own projects—writing to persuade, writing research pieces where we make our own evidence trails transparent. In science classes we can investigate local water quality in our communities. In art class we can consider perspective as we interpret artists' work. Developing these skills requires more than hit-or-miss pedagogy. Teachers, however, are often balancing myriad other demands on instructional time.

Yet we must find a way. If we want to prepare students to thoughtfully engage the world around them, not falling prey to whatever message lights up their phone, we must stay the course. A government of the people, for the people, and by the people demands nothing less.

NOTE

1. This lesson is one that I make sure parents are aware of. I want to be sure that they understand my intentions. The point is not to change anyone's mind, but that being informed means reading widely.

REFERENCES

Brown, M. W., & Weisgard, L. (1999). *The important book*. New York, NY: Harper Collins.

Cambridge Dictionary. (2018) Fake news. Retrieved from dictionary.cambridge.org/us/dictionary/english/fake-news

McGrew, S., Breakstone, J., Ortega, T., Smith, M., & Wineburg, S. (2018). Can students evaluate online sources? Learning from assessments of civic online reasoning. *Theory & Research in Social Education, 46*, 165–193.

National Council for the Social Studies. (2013). *College, Career and Civic Life (C3)*

Framework for Social Studies State Standards: Guidance for enhancing the rigor of K–12 civics, economics, geography, and history. Silver Spring, MD: Author.

National Council for the Social Studies. (2016). Media literacy. *Social Education, 80,* 183–185.

Rosenthal, A. K., & Lichtenheld, T. (2009). *Duck! Rabbit!* San Francisco, CA: Chronicle Books.

Afterword

Jeremy Stoddard

In the introduction to this volume Wayne Journell writes, "When individuals lose the willingness or ability to vet their political information, democracy is at risk." This statement sets the tone and context for the chapters that follow. It also, however, raises the question as to whether individuals have always had an issue vetting their political information. As many of the authors note, it is the context of political partisanship, social "sorting," prevalence of information overload, and effects of the "filter bubble" that is the culprit as much as any individual's capacity to evaluate political information.

This volume makes a contribution precisely because it moves us beyond the Currency, Relevance, Authority, Accuracy, and Purpose (CRAAP) test to examine the various reasons why teachers, students, and the public in general continue to lack the skills to evaluate information thoughtfully, or why they simply choose not to because of psychological, ideological, social, and technological influences. Basic skills and heuristics for evaluating information are only effective if they are examined within the political and social contexts of information and how we engage it.

Many chapters also provide logical next steps for attempting to help current teachers and their students who, while media savvy, often lack critical and reflective skills and habits. Finally, while these chapters are extraordinarily timely and valuable in their contribution and in painting a path forward, I also include in this afterword some potential ways forward on ideas not fully formed in this volume.

THE PROBLEM OF FAKE NEWS

As many of the authors note, the notion of "fake news" is not new, nor is it all about news. In Chapter 1 Garrett provides a useful taxonomy of the contemporary fake news phenomena: sensationalized stories used to generate clicks and therefore advertising dollars, disinformation being used for political purposes, and the use of the categorization of "fake news" to challenge and discredit any news source or story that is critical or misaligned with a particular political view (or anything with which President Trump disagrees).

One additional area touched upon by Hodgin and Kahne in their chapter expands upon this third type of "fake news." That is the use of the term to discredit legitimate journalism more universally, which is one of the outcomes cited by the RAND Corporation's report *Truth Decay* (Kavanagh & Rich, 2018).

Woodson, King, and Kim's chapter, and its emphasis on the power of information and who controls it historically, also evokes a parallel contemporary issue. If colonialism in the 17th and 18th centuries was shaped and maintained by tools of power such as the map, the census, and the museum (Anderson, 2006), then could the same be said about the tools of communication in the 20th and 21st centuries?

Communication tools, from powerful newspapers and their editors and owners to the Fox News Channel under former chairman Roger Ailes, have wielded great influence over politicians and the populace. The Internet was supposed to disrupt this power much in the way that Airbnb has disrupted the room rental market. As much as the World Wide Web has been a democratizing force, the powerful corporations and news organizations have fought back to maintain their dominance. However, this attempted disruption and correction has led to an explosion of information and news information outlets at the same time as people use other media tools (e.g., news apps) to help filter information, the so-called filter bubble (Pariser, 2011), which has contributed to the rise in partisanship.

One aspect of the fake news phenomena not explored in depth in this volume is the use of the fake news crisis by legacy news organizations, such as prominent newspaper organizations (e.g., *New York Times*) and foundations created by these organizations (e.g., Knight Foundation), to promote their own versions of news literacy programs for K–12 and higher education audiences. These educational programs emerged in the wake of the 2008 recession that served as a sort of death knell for many traditional newspapers, forcing them to consolidate in the face of rapidly dropping subscription levels.

These cuts meant the closing of many news bureaus in the United States and abroad, the laying off of reporters, and the shift to a model of journalism emphasizing advertising profits and a desire to post on newsworthy events quickly to compete with other sources. The news literacy programs, overall, promote quality programs emphasizing the kinds of analysis and corroboration of sources advocated for in this volume. However, these programs are also designed to place the legacy news organizations consistently at the top of the truth pyramid.

There is a case to be made that there is a wide range of quality in journalism, as Hodgin and Kahne note in Chapter 6, but these programs emphasize the objectivity of newspapers over other sources, including activist or citizen journalism. These newspaper-sponsored news literacy programs maintain that newspapers alone hold a level of truth that is verifiable and seemingly neutral. This emphasis on objectivity in journalism is a newer phenomenon (20th century) than the various forms of fake news—and in part may have laid the groundwork for the current assault on journalism by the Trump administration.

News organizations have historically been tied to particular political views, with many cities having conservative and liberal leaning papers that may sit juxtaposed on a newsstand—exposing any customer or walker-by to potential disagreements on issues through their varying headlines on stories, thus creating the kinds of crosscutting political exposure that political scientist Diana Mutz (2006) has noted is now much rarer. The key takeaway in all of this is that we need to help young people better evaluate information for quality but also recognize that these sources have a political voice and often a political interest.

The importance of both evaluation and student recognition of the political perspectives of information sources arises in Segall et al.'s chapter, as well as within the context of motivated reasoning identified by Hodgin and Kahne. Segall et al.'s chapter, in particular, examines the direct impact of students bringing inaccurate and/or highly partisan information into discussions of controversial issues. The impact of motivated reasoning, and the often-conscious effort in discussions to argue for your side versus engaging in seeking common understandings through disagreement, is clearly apparent in their study.

Their examples from a study of high school students illustrate the power that students can have in influencing each other on issues, particularly when information is introduced into a discussion or deliberation that is blatantly partisan or patently false but is viewed in the group as legitimate because others may be wary of countering their peers or do not have the tools to examine the evidence. This study makes the case for explicit and conscious incorporation of media education into democratic education. However, this goal is easier said than done, and it is also not a new issue (Mason, Krutka, & Stoddard, 2018; Stoddard, 2014).

HOW TO ADDRESS THE PROBLEM OF FAKE NEWS

In the early 2000s I worked as a curriculum and technology specialist for an educational services agency serving 35 school districts in Wisconsin. At that time, states were rapidly working to get fiber optic pipelines to every school district in the country to help combat the gap in access, and the use of the Internet in classrooms was becoming more ubiquitous. One of the professional development projects I led focused on integrating student research into the curriculum and had a heavy focus on information literacy.

Many teachers at that time were, at best, using some variation of what is now known as the CRAAP test as a heuristic for their students to evaluate web-based information. However, this heuristic still relies on the analysis of web-based sources such as the base URL (e.g., .edu, .org) as if they held some kind of objective marker of quality. In my workshops I would use the website of a Holocaust denier named Arthur Butz who was a professor of electrical engineering at Northwestern University. His site had the look of academic quality for the time, and it was often confused for a legitimate source—he was a professor and it had an ".edu" URL address.

In my workshops we would break down aspects of the URL to help better understand the basic architecture of the World Wide Web and an analysis of the source for key markers of expertise. This process included doing the kinds of "lateral reading" McGrew and her colleagues thoughtfully articulate in their chapter of this volume. I had participants search for information about Butz and look for corroborating evidence for aspects of the site that they found most questionable.

I include this example to make the point that the challenge fake news poses to the classroom teacher certainly includes the long history of propaganda and disinformation campaigns, but possibly even more problematic is the challenge of students who will quickly find and use sources with poor quality information produced by nonexperts (another high school class I worked with cited a project done by 4th-graders on simple machines!). It is also important to note that these heuristics were rarely used on traditional news sources as they had fostered an image of objectivity which, as noted above, is something that has been broken in the current context.

Chapters by Hauver, Hodgin and Kahne, and McGrew et al. provide strategies, sample updated heuristics, and tools for engaging students in the evaluation of evidence and placing news in context. Hauver's example activities, and in particular her examples of question sets for different new media sources and goals, provide a concrete model for engaging young students in evaluating information.

These question sets are influenced by media studies theorists such as Stuart Hall (2006) who encouraged us to examine text and context, author and intent, as well as preferred and alternative readings of any particular text. Similarly, the strategies outlined by Hodgin and Kahne, and those developed as assessments and practices by the Stanford History Education Group (McGrew et al.), treat websites and other forms of online information less like a static text akin to a primary source or piece of literature. It is, of course, always a balancing act between evaluating sources and viewing them as subjective in the slippery slope of a world without truth.

This space between objectivity and subjectivity also makes Hodgin and Kahne's emphasis on metacognition and helping students understand how engaging with these sources affects their views and what they know vastly important and worthy of further examination. They also make a key point of the need to examine the quality of sources and recognize the range of quality, while also noting that any news organization will have a particular perspective. Similarly, Middaugh's work with students in recognizing not only the importance of evaluation, but also the need to be more conscious of the actions they take with sharing social media, including political information, is an important contribution to the field.

HOW DO WE MOVE FORWARD FROM HERE?

One important trend in the intersection of media education and democratic education is the appropriation of disciplinary concepts, tools, and epistemic frames for both research and practice, which takes us beyond the textbook and allows for a more realistic examination of the role of media in politics and civic action. Building from Journell and Clark's chapter on memes, what other disciplinary tools—from media studies, political communications, political psychology, or communications—may be helpful, both for researchers and as models for designing curriculum and pedagogies?

Across these chapters, concepts such as motivated reasoning and confirmation bias are key for this work. What else is missing in the current civics and government curricula? For example, concepts such as earned media, or the free coverage of candidates and groups by various news organizations, seem to also be key for understanding the current political context. It is estimated, for example, that President Trump received up to five billion dollars in free coverage for his campaign (Stewart, 2016).

In addition to disciplinary tools, are young people learning about the media ecologies we inhabit and at least a modicum of how they function and are structured? Building from Hodgin and Kahne's chapter, how can we get students not only to engage in metacognition around their interpretation and engagement with texts, but also to reflect upon why they came across those sources in the first place? How can we engage students in recognizing their own actions, as well as the influence of social networks and technological functions of algorithms, that lead to what news they see and what they believe? What role does emotion play in these processes as students engage with, analyze, and use political information (e.g., Currie Sivek, 2018)?

Then, similar to Middaugh's work, how can we get students to more consciously seek out different views from quality sources? One element that could be a next step for the work in this volume is a closer examination of the technological elements and social structures that help fake news function so effectively (e.g., Cohen, 2018), as well as the ways in which we can engage students in more thoughtfully analyzing, deliberating, and engaging with news and political media.

REFERENCES

Anderson, B. (2006). *Imagined communities: Reflections on the origin and spread of nationalism.* London, United Kingdom: Verso.

Cohen, J. N. (2018). Exploring echo-systems: How algorithms shape immersive media environments." *Journal of Media Literacy Education, 10*(2), 139-151.

Currie Sivek, S. (2018). Both facts and feelings: Emotion and news literacy. *Journal of Media Literacy Education, 10*(2), 123-138.

Hall, S. (2006). Encoding/decoding. In M. Durham & D. Kellner (Eds.), *Media and cultural studies: Keyworks* (pp. 164–173). Oxford, United Kingdom: Blackwell.

Kavanagh, J., & Rich, M. D. (2018). *Truth decay: An initial exploration of the diminishing role of facts and analysis in American public life.* Santa Monica, CA: RAND Corporation. Available at www.rand.org/pubs/research_reports/RR2314.html

Mason, L. E., Krutka, D., & Stoddard, J. (2018). Media literacy, democracy, and the challenge of fake news. *Journal of Media Literacy Education, 10*(2), 1-10.

Mutz, D. (2006). *Hearing the other side: Deliberative versus participatory democracy.* Cambridge, United Kingdom: Cambridge University Press.

Pariser, E. (2011). *The filter bubble: How the new personalized Web is changing what we read and how we think.* London, United Kingdom: Penguin Books.

Stewart, E. (November 20, 2016). Donald Trump rode $5 billion in free media to the White House. *TheStreet.* Retrieved from www.thestreet.com/story/13896916/1/donald-trump-rode-5-billion-in-free-media-to-the-white-house.html

Stoddard, J. (2014). The need for media education in democratic education. *Democracy & Education, 22*(1). Retrieved from democracyeducationjournal.org/home/vol22/iss1/4

About the Editor and Contributors

Wayne Journell is an associate professor and secondary education program coordinator at the University of North Carolina at Greensboro. His research focuses on the teaching of politics and political processes in secondary education. He is the editor of two previous volumes, *Teaching Social Studies in an Era of Divisiveness: The Challenges of Discussing Social Issues in a Non-Partisan Way* and *Reassessing the Social Studies Curriculum: Promoting Critical Civic Engagement in a Politically Polarized, Post-9/11 World*, both published by Rowman & Littlefield in 2016. More recently, he authored *Teaching Politics in Secondary Education: Engaging with Contentious Issues* (SUNY Press, 2017). He currently serves as editor of *Theory & Research in Social Education*, which is the premier research journal in the field of social studies education, and he is a two-time recipient of the Exemplary Research in Social Studies Award from the National Council for the Social Studies (NCSS), as well as a recipient of the Early Career Award from the College and University Faculty Assembly of NCSS.

Joel Breakstone directs the Stanford History Education Group (SHEG). He received his PhD from the Stanford Graduate School of Education. Along with Mark Smith and Sam Wineburg, he led the development of SHEG's assessment website, Beyond the Bubble. He received the Larry Metcalf Exemplary Dissertation Award from the National Council for the Social Studies in 2014. He holds a BA in history from Brown University and an MA in Liberal Studies from Dartmouth College. After college, he taught high school history in Thetford, Vermont. His research focuses on how teachers use assessment data to inform instruction.

Christopher H. Clark is an assistant professor at Northeastern State University. His research focuses on student political thinking and identity. His work has been published in top journals such as *Theory & Research in Social Education* and *Teaching and Teacher Education.*

Margaret Smith Crocco is Professor and Chair of the Department of Teacher Education at Michigan State University. She has also served on the faculties of Teachers College, Columbia University and the University of Iowa. She taught American history, government, and women's studies for 8 years in New Jersey before becoming a teacher educator. She has authored or edited eight books, published in journals such as *Theory & Research in Social Education*, *Journal of Social Studies Research*, *Journal of Curriculum Studies*, and *History of Education Quarterly*, and done significant funded curriculum work related to films and novels, such as *When the Levees Broke* (Spike Lee), *Revolution '67* (Marylou & Jerome Bongiorno), and *When the Emperor Was Divine* (Julie Otsuka).

H. James Garrett is an associate professor at the University of Georgia in the Department of Educational Theory and Practice. His research centers on the emotional demands of learning and teaching about the social world. He is currently researching the emotional textures of classroom-based discussions of current social and political issues and also collaborates on a research team investigating social studies teachers' understandings and use of news media in their pedagogies.

Anne-Lise Halvorsen is an associate professor in the Department of Teacher Education at Michigan State University. Her research interests are elementary social studies education, historical inquiry, project-based learning, the history of education, the integration of social studies and literacy, and teacher preparation in the social studies. She is the author of *A History of Elementary Social Studies: Romance and Reality* (Peter Lang, 2013) and the coauthor of *Powerful Social Studies for Elementary Students* (Cengage, 2012). Anne-Lise was named the Michigan Council for the Social Studies College Educator of the Year in 2017. She is a former kindergarten teacher and a former curriculum writer for the State of Michigan.

Jennifer Hauver is Associate Professor of Education at Randolph-Macon College in Ashland, VA. Her scholarship focuses on democratic and civic learning in schools and communities. She is coauthor of *Religion in the Classroom: Dilemmas for Democratic Education* (Routledge, 2014) and coeditor of *Feminist Community Engagement: Achieving Praxis* (Palgrave MacMillan, 2014). She is currently at work on a book entitled *Young Children's Civic Mindedness: Using Research to Inform Practice* (Routledge).

Erica Hodgin is Associate Director of the Civic Engagement Research Group (CERG) at the University of California–Riverside. She is also Co-Principal Investigator with Joe Kahne of Educating for Democracy in the Digital Age—a districtwide civic education effort in partnership with Oakland Unified School District. Her current research focuses on the educational implications of youth civic and political engagement in the digital age. She has authored articles in *Theory & Research in Social Education* and the

Journal of Digital and Media Literacy, as well as several book chapters. Erica received her EdD in Educational Leadership from Mills College and completed her dissertation on the ways cultural humility can enable teachers to build effective relationships with students across racial and cultural differences. Before joining CERG, Erica taught English and social studies and served as an instructional coach at the middle school and high school levels.

Rebecca Jacobsen is an associate professor of education politics and policy in the College of Education at Michigan State University and Associate Director of the Education Policy Center. Her research examines how policies shape both opportunities for and barriers to civic and political engagement within the public education system. She has written extensively about the politics of accountability policies and whether and how schools prepare the next generation of citizens. Her work has been published in a number of journals, including *Teachers College Record, American Educational Research Journal, American Journal of Education,* and *Urban Affairs Review*. Her current work (with Jeff Henig and Sarah Reckhow) focuses on the changing nature of local school board election politics and the rise of large, outside campaign donations. Prior to graduate school, Rebecca taught elementary and middle school in the New York City public schools.

Joseph Kahne is the Ted and Jo Dutton Presidential Professor for Education Policy and Politics at the University of California–Riverside. He is also Chair of the MacArthur Foundation Research Network on Youth and Participatory Politics (YPP). Through this network, scholars from diverse disciplines examine ways participation with digital media is shaping and reshaping youth civic and political engagement. Professor Kahne's research and writing focuses on the influence of school practices and new media on youth civic and political development. Currently, with Cathy Cohen, he is Co-Principal Investigator of the YPP survey project. Scholarship from this project draws on a nationally representative survey of youth and examines engagement with new media and politics. He is also Co-Principal Investigator with Erica Hodgin of Educating for Democracy in the Digital Age—working with Oakland Unified School District and the National Writing Project on a districtwide civic education effort. Professor Kahne's articles have received outstanding paper of the year awards from the American Educational Research Association, the American Political Science Association Division of Teaching and Learning, and several other organizations. He sits on the steering committee of the National Campaign for the Civic Mission of Schools and on the advisory board of the Center for Information and Research on Civic Learning.

Esther Kim is a doctoral student in social studies education at the University of Texas–Austin. Her research focuses on the relationships between racial, religious, and civic identities. Prior to her graduate studies, she taught secondary World History and U.S. History in California and South Korea.

LaGarrett J. King is an assistant professor of social studies education at the University of Missouri. His research focus is on the teaching and learning of Black history in schools and society. His work has been published in *Theory & Research in Social Education*; *Social Education*; *Teaching Education*; *Urban Education*; *Race, Ethnicity, and Education*; and *Journal of Negro Education*.

Rebecca Klein is education news editor and primary education reporter for *HuffPost*, focusing on K–12 issues. Prior to working at *HuffPost,* she worked as a producer for National Public Radio affiliates in New York and Boston.

Sarah McGrew is a doctoral candidate in the Stanford Graduate School of Education where she codirects Stanford History Education Group's Civic Online Reasoning Project. She earned a BA in Political Science and Education from Swarthmore College before completing the Stanford Teacher Education Program (STEP). After STEP, she taught world history in Washington, DC. Her research focuses on teaching and assessing civic online reasoning in social studies classrooms.

Ellen Middaugh is an assistant professor of child and adolescent development in the Lurie College of Education at San José State University. Her research focuses on the influence of varied social contexts on youth civic identity development and on the implications of digital media for positive youth development. Recent publications include "Digital Media, Participatory Politics, and Positive Youth Development" in *Pediatrics* (Middaugh, Clark & Ballard, 2017) and "U Suk! Participatory Media and Youth Experiences with Political Discourse" in *Youth & Society* (Middaugh, Bowyer & Kahne, 2017). She previously served as Research Director for the Mills College Civic Engagement Research Group.

Teresa Ortega is the Stanford History Education Group's senior project manager and divides her time among research, curriculum development, and communications. She graduated from Stanford University in 2012 with a BA in history in the major's public history and public service track.

Avner Segall is a professor in the Department of Teacher Education at Michigan State University. His research, which uses the lenses of postmodernism, poststructuralism, feminism, and critical theory, focuses on secondary social studies education, public pedagogy, critical geography, and cultural studies.

His papers have appeared in journals such as *Teachers College Record, Curriculum Inquiry, Journal of Curriculum Studies, Teaching and Teacher Education*, and *Theory & Research in Social Education*. He is coauthor of *Christian Privilege in U.S. Education: Legacies and Current Issues* (Routledge, 2017) and *Beyond Pedagogy: Reconsidering the Public Purpose of Museums* (Sense, 2014).

Mark Smith is the Stanford History Education Group's (SHEG) Director of Assessment. Along with Joel Breakstone and Sam Wineburg, he led the development of SHEG's assessment website, Beyond the Bubble. He received a PhD from the Stanford Graduate School of Education in 2014 and also holds an MAT in secondary social studies education from the University of Iowa and a BA in history and political science from the University of Northern Iowa. Previously, he taught high school social studies in Cedar Rapids, Iowa; Plano, Texas; and Palo Alto, California. His research is focused on K–12 history assessment, particularly on issues of validity and generalizability.

Jeremy Stoddard is an associate professor in the Department of Curriculum & Instruction at the University of Wisconsin-Madison. His research focuses on the role of media in teaching and learning history and citizenship, engaging students in contemporary and historic controversial issues and events, and more generally on authentic pedagogy and assessment in classrooms and curriculum. His work has been published in journals such as *Teachers College Record, Curriculum Inquiry,* and *Theory & Research in Social Education*. His most recent book is *Teaching Difficult History Through Film* (Routledge, 2017)

Sam Wineburg is the Margaret Jacks Professor of Education and of History (by courtesy) at Stanford University and the founder and Executive Director of the Stanford History Education Group. He directs Stanford's PhD program in History Education and oversees the MA program for future history teachers. His scholarship has been featured in *The New York Times*, *The Washington Post*, *USA Today*, *The New Yorker*, and on National Public Radio and C-SPAN. In 2003 his book *Historical Thinking and Other Unnatural Acts: Charting the Future of Teaching the Past* (Temple University Press, 2001) received the Frederic W. Ness Award from the Association of American Colleges and Universities for the most important contribution to "improvement of Liberal Education and understanding the Liberal Arts." In 2007 he was awarded the American Historical Association's William Gilbert Prize for distinguished scholarship on the teaching of history as well as being named a Distinguished Lecturer by the Organization of American Historians.

Ashley N. Woodson is the Stauffer Faculty Fellow of Education and Assistant Professor of Education at the University of Missouri–Columbia. Her research examines the possibilities of critical race and queer pedagogies in urban social studies teacher education and the ways that Black adolescents draw on history to make sense of their everyday lives. She has published in the *Journal of Lesbian Studies*; *Urban Education*; *Social Education*; *Theory & Research in Social Education*; *Journal of Urban Learning, Teaching and Research*; and *Research on Human Development*.